GENGHIS KHAN

WORLD LEADERS PAST & PRESENT

GENGHIS KHAN

Judy Humphrey

CHELSEA HOUSE PUBLISHERS
PHILADELPHIA

EDITOR-IN-CHIEF: Nancy Toff
EXECUTIVE EDITOR: Remmel T. Nunn
MANAGING EDITOR: Karyn Gullen Browne
COPY CHIEF: Perry Scott King
ART DIRECTOR: Giannella Garrett

Staff for GENGHIS KHAN:

SENIOR EDITOR: John W. Selfridge
ASSISTANT EDITORS: Maria Behan, Pierre Hauser, Kathleen McDermott, Bert Yaeger
COPY EDITORS: Gillian Bucky, Sean Dolan
DESIGN ASSISTANT: Jill Goldreyer
PICTURE RESEARCH: Karen Herman
LAYOUT: Debbie Jay
PRODUCTION COORDINATOR: Alma Rodriguez
COVER ILLUSTRATION: Alan J. Nahigian

CREATIVE DIRECTOR: Harold Steinberg

Printed and bound in the United Stated of America.

Frontispiece courtesy of The Bettmann Archive

15 14 13

Library of Congress Cataloging in Publication Data

Humphrey, Judy. GENGHIS KHAN

(World leaders past & present)
Bibliography: p.
Includes index.
1. Genghis Khan, 1162–1227—Juvenile literature.
2. Mongols—Kings and rulers—Biography—Juvenile literature. 3. Mongolia—History—Juvenile literature.
[1. Genghis Khan, 1162–1227. 2. Kings, queens, rulers, etc.
3. Mongolia—History] I. Title. II. Series. World leaders past & present.
DS22.H86 1987 951′.702′0924 [B] [92] 87-5194

ISBN 0-87754-527-8
0-7910-0635-2 (pbk.)

Contents

"On Leadership," Arthur M. Schlesinger, jr. 7
1. A Land Awaiting Its Leader 13
2. The Boy Who Would Be Conqueror 23
3. The "Temporary" Khan 41
4. The Master of Mongolia 51
5. Order on the Steppes 61
6. The Mongol War Machine 77
7. The Final Battle 91
Further Reading 108
Chronology 109
Index 110

WORLD LEADERS PAST & PRESENT

John Adams
John Quincy Adams
Konrad Adenauer
Alexander the Great
Salvador Allende
Marc Antony
Corazon Aquino
Yasir Arafat
King Arthur
Hafez al-Assad
Kemal Atatürk
Attila
Clement Attlee
Augustus Caesar
Menachem Begin
David Ben-Gurion
Otto von Bismarck
Léon Blum
Simon Bolívar
Cesare Borgia
Willy Brandt
Leonid Brezhnev
Julius Caesar
John Calvin
Jimmy Carter
Fidel Castro
Catherine the Great
Charlemagne
Chiang Kai-shek
Winston Churchill
Georges Clemenceau
Cleopatra
Constantine the Great
Hernán Cortés
Oliver Cromwell
Georges-Jacques Danton
Jefferson Davis
Moshe Dayan
Charles de Gaulle
Eamon De Valera
Eugene Debs
Deng Xiaoping
Benjamin Disraeli
Alexander Dubček
François & Jean-Claude Duvalier
Dwight Eisenhower
Eleanor of Aquitaine
Elizabeth I
Faisal
Ferdinand & Isabella
Francisco Franco
Benjamin Franklin
Frederick the Great
Indira Gandhi
Mohandas Gandhi
Giuseppe Garibaldi
Amin & Bashir Gemayel
Genghis Khan
William Gladstone
Mikhail Gorbachev
Ulysses S. Grant
Ernesto "Che" Guevara
Tenzin Gyatso
Alexander Hamilton
Dag Hammarskjöld
Henry VIII
Henry of Navarre
Paul von Hindenburg
Hirohito
Adolf Hitler
Ho Chi Minh
King Hussein
Ivan the Terrible
Andrew Jackson
James I
Wojciech Jaruzelski
Thomas Jefferson
Joan of Arc
Pope John XXIII
Pope John Paul II
Lyndon Johnson
Benito Juárez
John Kennedy
Robert Kennedy
Jomo Kenyatta
Ayatollah Khomeini
Nikita Khrushchev
Kim Il Sung
Martin Luther King, Jr.
Henry Kissinger
Kublai Khan
Lafayette
Robert E. Lee
Vladimir Lenin
Abraham Lincoln
David Lloyd George
Louis XIV
Martin Luther
Judas Maccabeus
James Madison
Nelson & Winnie Mandela
Mao Zedong
Ferdinand Marcos
George Marshall
Mary, Queen of Scots
Tomáš Masaryk
Golda Meir
Klemens von Metternich
James Monroe
Hosni Mubarak
Robert Mugabe
Benito Mussolini
Napoléon Bonaparte
Gamal Abdel Nasser
Jawaharlal Nehru
Nero
Nicholas II
Richard Nixon
Kwame Nkrumah
Daniel Ortega
Mohammed Reza Pahlavi
Thomas Paine
Charles Stewart Parnell
Pericles
Juan Perón
Peter the Great
Pol Pot
Muammar el-Qaddafi
Ronald Reagan
Cardinal Richelieu
Maximilien Robespierre
Eleanor Roosevelt
Franklin Roosevelt
Theodore Roosevelt
Anwar Sadat
Haile Selassie
Prince Sihanouk
Jan Smuts
Joseph Stalin
Sukarno
Sun Yat-sen
Tamerlane
Mother Teresa
Margaret Thatcher
Josip Broz Tito
Toussaint L'Ouverture
Leon Trotsky
Pierre Trudeau
Harry Truman
Queen Victoria
Lech Walesa
George Washington
Chaim Weizmann
Woodrow Wilson
Xerxes
Emiliano Zapata
Zhou Enlai

CHELSEA HOUSE PUBLISHERS

ON LEADERSHIP

Arthur M. Schlesinger, jr.

LEADERSHIP, it may be said, is really what makes the world go round. Love no doubt smooths the passage; but love is a private transaction between consenting adults. Leadership is a public transaction with history. The idea of leadership affirms the capacity of individuals to move, inspire, and mobilize masses of people so that they act together in pursuit of an end. Sometimes leadership serves good purposes, sometimes bad; but whether the end is benign or evil, great leaders are those men and women who leave their personal stamp on history.

Now, the very concept of leadership implies the proposition that individuals can make a difference. This proposition has never been universally accepted. From classical times to the present day, eminent thinkers have regarded individuals as no more than the agents and pawns of larger forces, whether the gods and goddesses of the ancient world or, in the modern era, race, class, nation, the dialectic, the will of the people, the spirit of the times, history itself. Against such forces, the individual dwindles into insignificance.

So contends the thesis of historical determinism. Tolstoy's great novel *War and Peace* offers a famous statement of the case. Why, Tolstoy asked, did millions of men in the Napoleonic Wars, denying their human feelings and their common sense, move back and forth across Europe slaughtering their fellows? "The war," Tolstoy answered, "was bound to happen simply because it was bound to happen." All prior history predetermined it. As for leaders, they, Tolstoy said, "are but the labels that serve to give a name to an end and, like labels, they have the least possible connection with the event." The greater the leader, "the more conspicuous the inevitability and the predestination of every act he commits." The leader, said Tolstoy, is "the slave of history."

Determinism takes many forms. Marxism is the determinism of class. Nazism the determinism of race. But the idea of men and women as the slaves of history runs athwart the deepest human instincts. Rigid determinism abolishes the idea of human freedom—

the assumption of free choice that underlies every move we make, every word we speak, every thought we think. It abolishes the idea of human responsibility, since it is manifestly unfair to reward or punish people for actions that are by definition beyond their control. No one can live consistently by any deterministic creed. The Marxist states prove this themselves by their extreme susceptibility to the cult of leadership.

More than that, history refutes the idea that individuals make no difference. In December 1931 a British politician crossing Park Avenue in New York City between 76th and 77th Streets around 10:30 P.M. looked in the wrong direction and was knocked down by an automobile—a moment, he later recalled, of a man aghast, a world aglare: "I do not understand why I was not broken like an eggshell or squashed like a gooseberry." Fourteen months later an American politician, sitting in an open car in Miami, Florida, was fired on by an assassin; the man beside him was hit. Those who believe that individuals make no difference to history might well ponder whether the next two decades would have been the same had Mario Constasino's car killed Winston Churchill in 1931 and Giuseppe Zangara's bullet killed Franklin Roosevelt in 1933. Suppose, in addition, that Adolf Hitler had been killed in the street fighting during the Munich *Putsch* of 1923 and that Lenin had died of typhus during World War I. What would the 20th century be like now?

For better or for worse, individuals do make a difference. "The notion that a people can run itself and its affairs anonymously," wrote the philosopher William James, "is now well known to be the silliest of absurdities. Mankind does nothing save through initiatives on the part of inventors, great or small, and imitation by the rest of us—these are the sole factors in human progress. Individuals of genius show the way, and set the patterns, which common people then adopt and follow."

Leadership, James suggests, means leadership in thought as well as in action. In the long run, leaders in thought may well make the greater difference to the world. But, as Woodrow Wilson once said, "Those only are leaders of men, in the general eye, who lead in action. . . . It is at their hands that new thought gets its translation into the crude language of deeds." Leaders in thought often invent in solitude and obscurity, leaving to later generations the tasks of imitation. Leaders in action—the leaders portrayed in this series—have to be effective in their own time.

And they cannot be effective by themselves. They must act in response to the rhythms of their age. Their genius must be adapted, in a phrase of William James's, "to the receptivities of the moment." Leaders are useless without followers. "There goes the mob," said the French politician hearing a clamor in the streets. "I am their leader. I must follow them." Great leaders turn the inchoate emotions of the mob to purposes of their own. They seize on the opportunities of their time, the hopes, fears, frustrations, crises, potentialities. They succeed when events have prepared the way for them, when the community is awaiting to be aroused, when they can provide the clarifying and organizing ideas. Leadership ignites the circuit between the individual and the mass and thereby alters history.

It may alter history for better or for worse. Leaders have been responsible for the most extravagant follies and most monstrous crimes that have beset suffering humanity. They have also been vital in such gains as humanity has made in individual freedom, religious and racial tolerance, social justice, and respect for human rights.

There is no sure way to tell in advance who is going to lead for good and who for evil. But a glance at the gallery of men and women in *World Leaders—Past and Present* suggests some useful tests.

One test is this: Do leaders lead by force or by persuasion? By command or by consent? Through most of history leadership was exercised by the divine right of authority. The duty of followers was to defer and to obey. "Theirs not to reason why / Theirs but to do and die." On occasion, as with the so-called enlightened despots of the 18th century in Europe, absolutist leadership was animated by humane purposes. More often, absolutism nourished the passion for domination, land, gold, and conquest and resulted in tyranny.

The great revolution of modern times has been the revolution of equality. The idea that all people should be equal in their legal condition has undermined the old structure of authority, hierarchy, and deference. The revolution of equality has had two contrary effects on the nature of leadership. For equality, as Alexis de Tocqueville pointed out in his great study *Democracy in America*, might mean equality in servitude as well as equality in freedom.

"I know of only two methods of establishing equality in the political world," Tocqueville wrote. "Rights must be given to every citizen, or none at all to anyone . . . save one, who is the master of all." There was no middle ground "between the sovereignty of all and the absolute power of one man." In his astonishing prediction of 20th-century totalitarian dictatorship, Tocqueville explained how the revolution of equality could lead to the *"Führerprinzip"* and more terrible absolutism than the world had ever known.

But when rights are given to every citizen and the sovereignty of all is established, the problem of leadership takes a new form, becomes more exacting than ever before. It is easy to issue commands and enforce them by the rope and the stake, the concentration camp and the *gulag.* It is much harder to use argument and achievement to overcome opposition and win consent. The Founding Fathers of the United States understood the difficulty. They believed that history had given them the opportunity to decide, as Alexander Hamilton wrote in the first Federalist Paper, whether men are indeed capable of basing government on "reflection and choice, or whether they are forever destined to depend . . . on accident and force."

Government by reflection and choice called for a new style of leadership and a new quality of followership. It required leaders to be responsive to popular concerns, and it required followers to be active and informed participants in the process. Democracy does not eliminate emotion from politics; sometimes it fosters demagoguery; but it is confident that, as the greatest of democratic leaders put it, you cannot fool all of the people all of the time. It measures leadership by results and retires those who overreach or falter or fail.

It is true that in the long run despots are measured by results too. But they can postpone the day of judgment, sometimes indefinitely, and in the meantime they can do infinite harm. It is also true that democracy is no guarantee of virtue and intelligence in government, for the voice of the people is not necessarily the voice of God. But democracy, by assuring the right of opposition, offers built-in resistance to the evils inherent in absolutism. As the theologian Reinhold Niebuhr summed it up, "Man's capacity for justice makes democracy possible, but man's inclination to injustice makes democracy necessary."

A second test for leadership is the end for which power is sought. When leaders have as their goal the supremacy of a master race or the promotion of totalitarian revolution or the acquisition and exploitation of colonies or the protection of greed and privilege or the preservation of personal power, it is likely that their leadership will do little to advance the cause of humanity. When their goal is the abolition of slavery, the liberation of women, the enlargement of opportunity for the poor and powerless, the extension of equal rights to racial minorities, the defense of the freedoms of expression and opposition, it is likely that their leadership will increase the sum of human liberty and welfare.

Leaders have done great harm to the world. They have also conferred great benefits. You will find both sorts in this series. Even "good" leaders must be regarded with a certain wariness. Leaders are not demigods; they put on their trousers one leg after another just like ordinary mortals. No leader is infallible, and every leader needs to be reminded of this at regular intervals. Irreverence irritates leaders but is their salvation. Unquestioning submission corrupts leaders and demeans followers. Making a cult of a leader is always a mistake. Fortunately hero worship generates its own antidote. "Every hero," said Emerson, "becomes a bore at last."

The signal benefit the great leaders confer is to embolden the rest of us to live according to our own best selves, to be active, insistent, and resolute in affirming our own sense of things. For great leaders attest to the reality of human freedom against the supposed inevitabilities of history. And they attest to the wisdom and power that may lie within the most unlikely of us, which is why Abraham Lincoln remains the supreme example of great leadership. A great leader, said Emerson, exhibits new possibilities to all humanity. "We feed on genius. . . . Great men exist that there may be greater men."

Great leaders, in short, justify themselves by emancipating and empowering their followers. So humanity struggles to master its destiny, remembering with Alexis de Tocqueville: "It is true that around every man a fatal circle is traced beyond which he cannot pass; but within the wide verge of that circle he is powerful and free; as it is with man, so with communities."

1

A Land Awaiting Its Leader

> ***They appear where least expected.***
> —GRIGOR OF AKANC
> Armenian monk, on the Mongols

The fierce young Mongol chieftain known as Yesugei the Brave was hunting alone on horseback, his hawk perched on his wrist, on that fateful summer day more than 800 years ago. As he neared the edge of the woods along the bank of the Onon River, he saw a well-dressed young horseman whom he recognized as a Merkit, a forest dweller from the north. Beside the rider was the most beautiful woman Yesugei had ever seen; she was driving a horse-drawn wagon loaded with possessions. Yesugei realized that the young couple were newlyweds, making their way back to the husband's people after wedding festivities with the family of the bride.

Yesugei's face grew hot as he gazed from the protection of the woods at the slim girl in her revealing short smock. Instantly, the strong-willed young man decided he must have her for himself, regardless of the consequences.

He rushed back to his camp, having shrewdly decided to enlist the help of two of his brothers. Soon the three men were galloping back to the river, bows and arrows at hand, their black braids streaming behind them.

A present-day Mongol chieftain holds his son. Yesugei the Brave, father of Genghis Khan, was chieftain of his own Mongol clan and descended from a long line of warrior chiefs.

AP/WIDE WORLD PHOTOS

Yesugei and his brothers grew up bold, dangerous, and poised for instant action. If they saw anything they wanted, they were inclined to think they had a right to it.

—R. P. LISTER
historian

The unfortunate couple had just crossed a shallow part of the river, and watched in horror as the horsemen approached. The girl had tears in her eyes as she looked up at her husband, but her voice was firm when she spoke. "You must flee; there are other women for you if you only will stay alive," said this courageous and practical woman. "But when you find another wife, please call her Hoelun, in remembrance of me." Then she slipped off her shift and gave it to him for a keepsake. Her husband put it inside his tunic, next to his skin, and rode away into the valley.

Although Yesugei and his brothers chased the Merkit for hours over the grassy hills, they could not catch up. At last they returned to where Hoelun sat crying on the wooden cart, her head on the folded felt tent in which she and her husband had planned to live. In Mongol legends it is said that she wept with such abandon that her breath stirred the waters of the Onon and fluttered the leaves in the forest.

The young bride who was so cruelly stolen from her husband was the mother of the great Genghis Khan.

Although the story lives in Mongol legend, the tale is a true one and perfectly illustrates the fierce world of Genghis Khan, the barbarian genius who conquered nearly all of Asia.

Even the setting of the saga is highly dramatic. In the center of the continent the sense of the vastness of the land is overwhelming, and indeed the ocean is thousands of miles away in any direction. The country is a study in contrasts: magnificent mountain ranges, dense forests, great rivers and lakes, endless expanses of grassy plains known as the steppes, and bare desert. In the spring the green grassland stretches to the horizon, but such gentleness is fleeting. A scorching sun burns the plains yellow by the middle of July; by October winter blizzards sweep in. For the next five months, all waterways are frozen. The temperature swings violently on many days during the year — from 45°F to 101°F in Mongolia's modern-day capital, Ulan Bator, for example. All year round the land is swept by winds

SOVFOTO

Ulan Bator, the capital of contemporary Mongolia, is situated 150 miles south of Genghis Khan's birthplace. Mountain ranges abruptly rise from the deserts and grassy flat steppes of this vast, harsh land.

that, in the words of one historian, "can almost lift a rider from his saddle."

From early ages to the time of Genghis Khan, the central part of this mighty land had been inhabited by three main groups of people sharing a common origin: the Tunguses, who hunted and fished in the East Siberian forests; Turks, who tilled the soil, worked with iron, and also raised cattle; and the Mongols, who became the wandering keepers of small herds of cattle, sheep, and horses. That the Mongols led their difficult nomadic life in such a vast, harsh land is testimony to their resilience and resourcefulness.

Among the many skills essential to the tribesmen's survival was their highly honed memory, which allowed them to navigate the miles not with instruments but according to the precisely remembered position of trees and the smallest stones, the stars, the flight of wild geese and cranes.

Although apparently given to understandable bouts of gloom, for the most part these nomads were high-spirited survivors. They loved feasting and drinking during the brief days of relative plenty — in early summer, when the grass was still green and

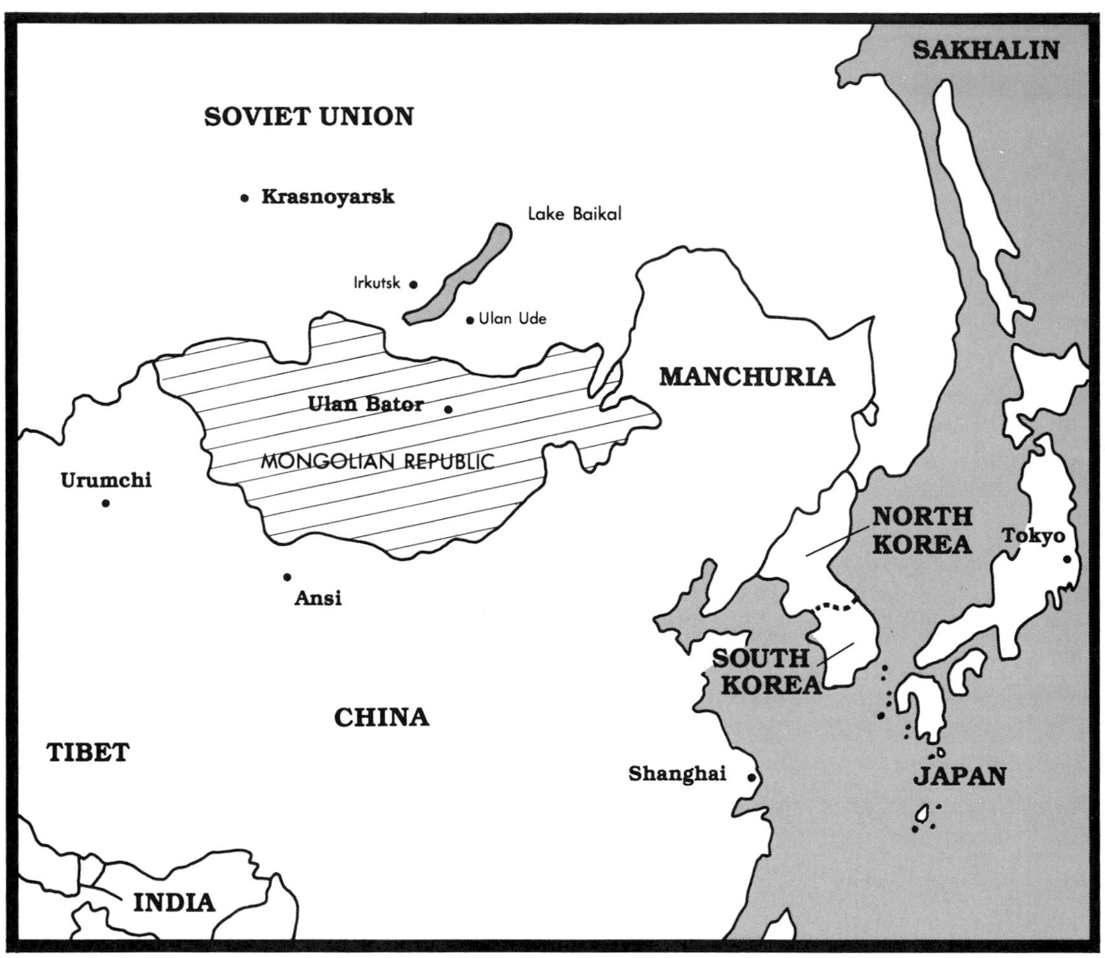

Modern Mongolia is dwarfed by its massive neighbors, the Soviet Union and China. During Genghis Khan's lifetime, the Mongol Empire included considerable amounts of territory from these two nations.

the mares were giving the nourishing milk that was a staple of the Mongol diet. They often spoke in a poetic style, and through countless generations they sang of their traditions, their legends, their codes of behavior, and above all, of the joys of hunting and battle and of their beautiful light-skinned women. There was no need to learn to write anything down.

Their appearance was fittingly rough-hewn: they were short (seldom taller than 5 feet 6 inches), with big bones, massive chests, and bowed legs from a life spent on horseback. Their faces were flat, with piercing brown or black eyes above high cheekbones, and when they grinned they displayed flashing white teeth. The men had little facial hair but grew sparse beards and arranged their wiry black hair in long plaits that hung down their backs.

These formidable-looking nomads were perfectly teamed with their most highly prized possessions, the sturdy Mongolian ponies that could carry them through storms of swirling snow or burning sand, survive the arid wastes of the Gobi Desert in the south, climb massive mountains, or travel for days across the steppes.

The nomads saw their lives as a constant battle against man, against evil spirits that lurked on earth, against poverty and the threat of starvation. Genghis Khan's people roamed the plains, dependent on their beasts, their own survival skills (including awesome hunting abilities), and on trade with people who lived in towns and villages near rivers and oases. Goods for trade were extremely scarce. The nomads exchanged horses, sheep, goats, meat, wool, and furs for corn, carpets, embroidered material, and iron, which was used for

Sturdy portable tents made of felt and wood provide nomadic Mongols their only shelter from extremes of heat and cold. As in the days of Genghis Khan, modern nomads engage in a constant struggle against poverty and their land's harsh climate.

AP/WIDE WORLD PHOTOS

CULVER PICTURES

The arid wastes of the Gobi Desert stretch for thousands of miles between China and Mongolia. Genghis Khan's armies crossed part of the harsh Gobi to invade China.

lances, arrowheads, and cooking utensils. Because the people were so desperately poor they stole whenever they could — or, if they were sufficiently strong and well organized, they waged war.

The fierce, harsh 12th-century world of Yesugei and Hoelun was in many ways similar to that of their distant ancestors. At least two millenia before, nomadic cattle breeders moved to and fro across the Mongolian plateau and central Asian steppes, in keeping with the changing colors of the grasslands. Records dating back as far as the 8th century B.C., when China was made up of loosely associated feudal states, tell of the invasion of those territories by Mongol barbarians from the north. By the 3rd century B.C. China was united as a military state, and an emperor was able to order that all the protective walls that had been built by individual princes around their lands be connected to keep out the marauders. The result was the remarkable Great Wall of China, nearly 2,000 miles long and wide enough for six horsemen to ride abreast on the top.

It was designed to keep northern China safe from the nomad hordes, but within a few decades barbarian tribes crossed even that mighty fortification.

> ***With a lion's strength they have voices more shrill than an eagle.***
>
> —GRIGOR OF AKANC
> Armenian monk, on the Mongols

Although the nomads were driven back in those ancient days, they gathered new followers in the course of their flight, conquered all the settled areas in their path, and pressed into new pasturelands, as eager for grazing land as for loot. During all these wanderings the various peoples were warring constantly among themselves for land, livestock, and possessions. Thus, for century after century until the rise of Genghis Khan, no central organization existed in Asia, and powerful leaders rose and fell in the unending struggle between the nomads and the settled people.

At the time Yesugei abducted Hoelun, medieval Europe — with its Gothic architecture, monks, knights, castles, and moats — was in full flower. Christianity was the unifying cultural force, and the Crusades to recover the Holy Land from Islam were well under way. The idealistic spirit of the time was exemplified by the prevailing tradition of chivalry, which extolled the virtues of bravery, loyalty, piety, and honor. Also flourishing was the feudal system, in which all land was vested in the king and held by a hierarchy of nobles, down to individual manor lords who oversaw the workers. The typical warrior was the knight. Protective guilds, or organizations of people engaged in the same business or craft, were another feature of the order-loving era. Everywhere commerce and industry were beginning to thrive.

Compare this well-organized, geographically compact society to the chaotic state of affairs in Asia, where frontiers were immense and communications weak. Goods were plundered not only from the interior cities but also from caravans traveling via such long-established trade routes as those through central Asia to the Black Sea and through present-day Iran to the Persian Gulf.

Ironically, at the time that Genghis's father stole Hoelun from her husband, much of Asia was considerably more advanced than Europe — in its magnificent art; in its science, philosophy, and

THE BETTMANN ARCHIVE

The Great Wall of China was built in the 3rd century B.C. to protect northern China from nomad invasions. Even this long, formidable barrier was unable to halt Genghis Khan's relentless advance against China's Qin Empire.

literature; and in its splendid towns, with their exquisite tiled buildings, their fountains and formal gardens, and their colleges. But the empires were decaying — particularly the Khwarezmian Empire in central Asia, which lay to the west of the Mongols, and the Qin Empire to the southeast, in China.

The Mongol society was in disarray as well. One difficulty stemmed from the fact that men were prohibited from marrying within their own clan, and since finding suitable wives was often difficult, raiding and kidnapping were common. Such acts often were followed by fierce blood feuds and reprisals.

Now, too, when a clan was defeated its people were enslaved, and every clan had slaves that originally belonged to other tribes, adding to the general unrest and disunity.

Still another problem was the breakdown of family

and blood ties. The society had always been based on patriarchal clans divided into closely knit families, yet respect for authority and mutual trust were on the wane. Partly for this reason families began breaking into fragments and moving on.

Clans were also splintering because the spoils of war now went not to the tribe at large but to its various warrior lords. When a lord acquired sufficient animals and men, he proceeded to leave and form a clan of his own. Yesugei, who was perhaps 20 years old when he captured his wife, was just such an adventurer.

These new lords of the steppe had to constantly try to consolidate their power by attracting new members for their tribe, fighting and acquiring slaves, and training a band of warriors. Even when the so-called prince, or *noyon*, was relatively powerful, he was obliged to struggle to provide for all his followers and thus had to wage war ever more vigorously. Brute force was the only law in the land; violence and conflict were a way of life.

Though the ancient patriarchal order was crumbling, a stable new system had yet to emerge. Thus it was that on the strife-ridden steppes and across the sprawling, troubled continent, the time was exactly right for the coming of a great leader.

2

The Boy Who Would be Conqueror

The pleasure and joy of man lies in treading down the rebel and conquering the enemy, in tearing him up by the root, in taking from him all that he has.
—GENGHIS KHAN

As Yesugei the Brave and his brothers took the beautiful, high-spirited Hoelun back to their camp, she continued to cry loudly for the husband they had driven away. Yesugei seemed willing to tolerate the noise, but one of the other men finally could stand it no longer. "Come, be quiet, woman," he urged, and pointed out that the one she wanted to hold again in her arms was already far away and would never come back.

For her own safety Hoelun decided to make the best of her plight and transfer her devotion to her captor. Yesugei in turn made Hoelun his chief wife — an honor that must have astonished her, considering the unceremonious way she and Yesugei had come together. According to the custom of the time, a man might have as many wives as he could support (most nomads, of course, could manage but one). No matter how many women a Mongol married, however, only one could be the wife who would bear her husband's heirs. When Yesugei married Hoelun, he already had two sons, Bektor and Belgutai, by a lesser wife. But his true children would be the four sons and the daughter he would eventually have by Hoelun.

Modern Mongol horsewomen. Traditionally, women have played an important role in Mongol society. The courage and tenacity of Genghis Khan's mother, Hoelun, enabled the family to survive great hardship.

AP/WIDE WORLD PHOTOS

The life of the remarkable Genghis Khan began in 1162 with what appeared to be an omen. When the infant entered the world, he was clutching a huge blood clot in his tiny fist. It shone like a dark jewel, and a wise man of the clan declared it a sign that the handsome baby would grow up to be a heroic warrior.

Yesugei was away fighting Mongol tribes called Tatars at the time of the birth, but late that night he returned with two captive enemy princes and many valuable possessions. When he saw his son, he called him Temujin, the name of the mightier of the enemy chiefs. According to an ancient custom, important men named their sons in commemoration of significant events at the time of their birth. The Mongols believed that the tradition ensured that their highly regarded male children would get off to a good start in life — an important consideration since the sons of nomad leaders would one day be responsible for protecting and supporting the other clan members.

As it happened, the name Temujin, which meant "iron worker," was well suited to the future "man of iron" who eventually would conquer the Asian world.

Two years after Temujin's birth a second son, Kasar, arrived; next came Khaji'un and Temuga, followed by a daughter who was named Temulin.

By the time Temujin, the future Genghis Khan, was 13, people had already begun to remark on his catlike "eyes of fire," which fixed on people with an unusually intense gaze. There was comment, too, on the "bright power" in his face; he was exceptionally alert and vigorous, with a tremendous energy animating his expressions.

Yesugei decided that it was time for the boy, as befitted the son of a worthy leader, to have a fiancée, and so he and Temujin rode to the southeast, in the direction of China, to find a suitable girl in Hoelun's tribe. The nomads believed that a chieftain's sons should marry outside the tribe to keep the ruling stock robust and to create new alliances on the dangerous steppes. Any family certainly would be proud to include Temujin among its members.

THE BETTMANN ARCHIVE

Temujin was named after a captured Tatar chieftain. This 18th-century engraving of Tatar life depicts the peaceful side of the warrior people responsible for Yesugei's death.

The journey was a long one for the young boy. He was accustomed to making winter and summer migrations with his people across the lush valleys that lay between thickly forested mountains, but now he found himself in a strange land with little grass. Huge black rocks jutted from the ground, and a fierce wind howled through the crags and ravines. Temujin and Yesugei were approaching the Great Wall of China, the northern boundary of the Qin Empire. Hoelun's people lived just north of the Wall.

Before they reached her relatives, however, they stopped beside the shore of a lake, where they saw grass for their horses and hoped to shoot game with their arrows. As Yesugei was roaming through the area on foot, he met Dai Sechen, a powerful chieftain whose tribe had grown wealthy through trade with Chinese merchants. Temujin must have been impressed with the fine fabrics, polished weapons, carved ivory, and beautiful ornaments that he eventually saw in Dai Sechen's *yurt*, or tent, where the old man told stories of wealthy cities beyond the Great Wall. Perhaps the impressionable child, poor in comparison to Dai Sechen, fantasized about having such riches for himself.

In any event, after Dai Sechen offered the travelers refreshment, he asked Yesugei where they were headed. Yesugei explained that they were seeking a girl for Temujin from among the Olhonod clan, the boy's maternal relatives. Dai Sechen studied the handsome boy and commented that Yesugei's son had fire in his glance and a glowing countenance. Then he described a dream he had had the night before, in which a white falcon holding the sun and the moon in its talons flew down from the heavens and perched on his wrist. The dream meant that

ART RESOURCE/GIRAUDON

A statue from the Qin dynasty. Temujin first learned of the Qin's rich civilization from his father-in-law, who traded with Chinese merchants. As Genghis Khan, he would eventually defeat the Qin Empire.

good fortune was on its way, Dai Sechen said — and here were two visitors to prove it.

Yesugei listened closely as the cunning old chieftain explained that his tribe was famous for its beautiful women, who bore fine sons. The females in the tribe were never sold for profit or given in exchange for land and servants, as often happened elsewhere, he said. Instead, they were simply raised to be worthy of marriage to chieftains and were a source of great pride to all. In fact, said Dai Sechen, leaders throughout the land sought out his tribe because of its lovely, smooth-cheeked girls.

"My daughter Bortei is only 14 — a year older than your Temujin," said Dai Sechen. "Come into my tent and meet her."

Yesugei saw that the child was exceptionally beautiful, and he requested her hand in marriage for Temujin. Dai Sechen readily agreed, of course, asking only that Temujin be left there in his camp until it was time for him to marry and return to his own clan — a common practice in those times. Boys who were betrothed often were reared by their future inlaws.

Both men were pleased with the arrangement. Yesugei would not need to travel farther to find a match for his firstborn, and the boy could remain in comparative security. That part of the continent was less savage than Yesugei's own land, and Temujin would be well cared for by the powerful chieftain. Dai Sechen was delighted, too. Now he was allied with a man who led a relatively powerful group of Mongols, and he had a most promising prospective son-in-law who, by all appearances, would grow into a man strong in both body and mind.

Dai Sechen held a great feast to celebrate the betrothal. Afterward Yesugei said good-bye to his son, and probably caught up in the emotion of the moment and searching for some final suggestion that might ensure his son's happiness, he blurted a warning to Dai Sechen not to allow Temujin to be frightened by any dogs!

As Yesugei made his way home, however, his fortunes suddenly changed. Whom should he encounter feasting around a campfire but a group of Tatars, who had been his enemies even before he captured two of their princes the day of Temujin's birth. The law of the steppe dictated that they must offer him food and drink and that he should accept their hospitality, so Yesugei dismounted and sat among them. They recognized him immediately, however, and put a slow-acting poison in his food. Yesugei did not begin to feel ill until he was on his way home, but by the time he reached his tent three days later, he was in excruciating pain and nearly blind.

Terrified because death was near but thinking of the well-being of the family that would soon be helpless without him, Yesugei gasped out a request for his faithful servant Munlik to be brought in. "What is to become of my children and all those I leave behind — my brothers, my widow, my sisters-in-law?" he lamented. "Munlik, go quickly and bring back my son!" he cried.

Those were the last words of Yesugei the Brave — and they marked the end of the childhood of Genghis Khan. At the age of 13 Temujin was catapulted fatherless into the brutal daily struggle for survival that constituted life in the Mongolian forests and steppes.

The faithful Munlik made his way across the many miles to Dai Sechen's camp. He was shrewd, however, and didn't tell the old chieftain about the tragedy that had occurred. Dai Sechen might have refused to give up the child had he known that Yesugei was dead. So Munlik said only that Yesugei missed his son badly and that he wished him to return home for a visit.

Although the request was unusual, the chieftain didn't want to anger Yesugei and so permitted Temujin to leave, on the condition that he be brought back again quickly.

Thus it was that Temujin returned to his people not as a grown man come to claim his rightful place but as a boy with no power whatsoever among the tribal contenders. Because he was a possible successor to his father's place, he was a threat to the men of the tribe. With Yesugei's death the clans that the chieftain had united because of his superiority as a warrior and hunter separated and were unable

AP/WIDE WORLD PHOTOS

A Mongol mother carries her child on her back. Marriages between clans were arranged by the parents of young children. After they became engaged, boys were often reared by their future wives' families.

to agree on who should lead them all. The camp was in chaos: violent quarrels erupted and the women argued among themselves. This unsettled state reflected in miniature the larger situation in the Mongol lands, whose people were unable to find a ruler who could hold them together for the common good.

Hoelun was treated respectfully for a time, but eventually the people in the camp went off in groups to the summer pastures, leaving her alone and defenseless with her four sons, her two stepsons, her daughter, and an old woman servant. Only one of the clansmen sided with Hoelun and tried to persuade the others to turn back. "The deep water is dried up," he was told then. "The bright stone is broken."

The loyal old man was the father of Munlik, who had brought Temujin back home from Dai Sechen's camp. When he continued to urge his people to return to Hoelun, one man drove his lance deep into the old man's spine. Somehow he managed to crawl back to his tent, where he lay dying. When Temujin heard what had happened he rushed to the old man's side, crying in rage and sorrow. Similar affection and gratitude for loyal subjects surfaced again and again in Genghis Khan over the years. The man is often portrayed only as a brutal savage, and certainly his ferocity toward his enemies knew no bounds; but he was unfailingly generous to those who were loyal to him, and in all dealings with his own people he scrupulously adhered to his own principles.

Hoelun, who had acted with such selflessness and courage 14 years earlier when she urged her young husband to save himself from Yesugei and his brothers, showed nobility and strength in this latest crisis. She took up the horsetail banner of the clan, galloped after the tribes, and ordered them to follow

THE BETTMANN ARCHIVE

This engraving depicts Genghis Khan as a ferocious warrior. Because of the early hardships he endured after the death of his father, the young Temujin learned to value strength and loyalty. His violence was tempered by the generosity he showed to his supporters.

> ***Death does not appear among them, for they survive for 300 years.***
>
> —GRIGOR OF AKANC
> Armenian monk, on the Mongols

her to the summer pasture. Many did rally around her for a day or two, but eventually they deserted her again, and she found herself alone in the camp except for seven children, one old woman, horses, and a few other animals. Undaunted, Hoelun spent every daylight hour of the summer walking up and down the banks of the Onon, gathering and bringing back to camp what food she could find — wild apples, berries, garlic, onions and other edible roots. The little group did not eat well, living as they did on food that was detested by most Mongols, but they survived that first summer and the next winter, too.

Temujin learned to hunt for rodents, and as time went on, the older boys became skilled at catching fish. The clansmen who had deserted Hoelun and her family must have assumed that the nine would starve or die from exposure in the harsh climate or be killed by other clans, but the women and children were truly of the Mongol race of iron. The children grew tall and cunning and strong as they hunted and played their games of war.

When the boys were well into adolescence, a terrifying tragedy occurred, perhaps triggered by brutal passions bred during long years of hardship and by rivalry between Yesugei's four sons by Hoelun and the two by his lesser wife.

The scene was a sunny riverbank where Temujin, his brother Kasar, and their half brothers Bektor and Belgutai were fishing with hooks bent from Hoelun's precious supply of needles, which she had obtained through trade in better days. Together Temujin, who was about 15, and Kasar, then 13, landed a beautiful trout. When Bektor and Belgutai, who were older and stronger, saw the prize fish, they immediately seized it and ran away.

Temujin and his brother hurried home and complained bitterly to Hoelun, but thinking only of the welfare of the clan, she scolded them for quarreling and urged them to make peace in order to save their anger for revenge on Yesugei's former followers.

The young boys were outraged; only the day before, their half brothers had stolen a lark from them, and now their fish was gone, as well. Taking their bows in hand, they rushed out to avenge themselves. When they spotted Bektor sitting on the riverbank, enjoying the remains of their fish, they circled around and crept up on him. Then they drew their bows, shot him, and returned to their mother's tent.

> ***Men killed each other for self-preservation, or out of a desire for power or wealth, or in a fit of sheer temper, but small boys rarely killed each other for a fish.***
>
> —R. P. LISTER
> historian, on
> Bektor's murder

Hoelun immediately knew from her sons' expressions what they had done, and she shouted at them, accusing them of behaving like the most voracious and savage of animals, calling them murderers.

The terrible deed demonstrates the ferocity of which Genghis Khan was capable even at an early age; murder of a close relative by one so young was unusual among the Mongols. By killing Bektor, Temujin had removed a constant source of trouble. Bektor was the only person who had ever really stood up to the self-possessed Temujin, and Belgutai alone would be no problem. One historian notes that Temujin gave Belgutai many presents after Bektor's death and won a faithful follower who would remain loyal always. Internal peace did eventually come to the little camp, and Temujin's authority remained unchallenged there. At the tender age of 15 Temujin had established himself as the head of his ragtag clan.

Two more years passed, and Hoelun and her children continued to fend for themselves on the cruel steppes. They became increasingly strong and shrewd, as if all the survival skills and instincts of their ancestors had been distilled and made more potent by the unique hardships they endured. Although the tiny group lived in wretched isolation for the most part, they were occasionally observed by passing nomads. Gradually the word spread across the steppes that not only had the nucleus of Yesugei's clan survived but that the children who had been left with their mother to die were developing into lean young wolves of the wild. The taletellers were especially taken with Temujin, who at 17 was tall and muscular, with fierce feline eyes, a proud bearing, and a face that radiated authority.

Targutai, the chieftain who was responsible for the clan's desertion of Hoelun and her brood, realized that the iron-willed wife of Yesugei the Brave

AP/WIDE WORLD PHOTOS

This 20th-century Mongol warrior exhibits the same fierce gaze mentioned in contemporary descriptions of Temujin, whose name meant "iron worker."

would be determined to avenge her family—and that her sons were old enough to carry out her wishes. But Targutai was too clever to consider killing these enemies. Yesugei had left many kinsmen in the land, and murdering his chief wife and his heirs might invite retribution. Targutai knew that Kasar, Temuga, Khaji'un, and Belgutai were ordinary youths who might become chieftains but would never be dangerous. Temujin, on the other hand, already had a reputation as one who had to be obeyed or forever feared. Targutai decided to storm Hoelun's camp with a band of horsemen and take Temujin prisoner. The others, he decided, could continue their sorry lives.

When the warriors reached the little camp they shouted for Temujin, but he had been warned and had fled to the forest, where he hid for nine days with nothing to eat but a few wild berries. Rather than starve quietly and in solitude, the exhausted youth resolved to at least die in action against Targutai's waiting warriors, and he led his horse out of the woods and feebly attempted to mount. The warriors immediately seized him.

Targutai's men took Temujin to their camp and placed a heavy wooden yoke around his neck and shoulders. Both his hands were fastened to the yoke so that he was in constant discomfort and entirely under the control of his captors. To further humiliate the proud Temujin, a youth no older than himself was assigned to guard him.

For day after weary day Temujin lived under the watchful eye of Targutai, who ordered that he eat and sleep in a different tent each night so that he wouldn't have a chance to win anyone over to his cause.

One summer evening, after the entire camp had been eating and drinking at a great ceremonial fes-

Mongol children learn hunting and survival skills at a very early age. While still a boy the resourceful Temujin hid from Targutai's warriors for nine days before he was captured.

EASTFOTO

tival on the banks of the river Onon, all the men retired to their tents to sleep. An exceptionally slim and weak-looking youth had taken his regular guard's place for the night. As soon as darkness fell, Temujin swung on the guard, struck him, and ran away to the river, where he hid in the reeds with only his head above the cold water. The guard roused himself and called for help, and the clanspeople, groggy from too much food, drink, and sleep, staggered from their tents and began a search. One of the men, Sorgan Shira, had known and respected Yesugei the Brave years before. When he suddenly saw the boy's face above the water near some rushes, he said in a low voice that no one but Temujin could hear: "It is for your far-seeing intelligence, for the fire in your eyes, for the light in your countenance that they hound you. Do not move. I shall not denounce you." Later, Sorgan Shira told the boy when he could safely climb out.

Although the kind man — who was understandably afraid of getting caught — urged Temujin to make his way to his mother's camp, Temujin knew that he could never get across the river and steppes wearing the heavy yoke. He thus decided to wait in the cold water until late in the night; then he crept to Sorgan Shira's tent.

Although Sorgan Shira was appalled at the sight of Temujin, since he would be executed if the fugitive were found in his tent, he and his sons nevertheless helped free Temujin from the wooden yoke and put it in the fire, which fortunately was necessary on the cool nights of the first month of summer. Then they hid him in a cartload of wool for three days. When the search subsided somewhat, Sorgan Shira gave him a mare, milk and lamb's meat, and bows and arrows.

Temujin never forgot Sorgan Shira's kindness, and when he became khan, he gave the man land, servants, and special privileges, and he made Sorgan Shira's sons generals in his army.

Although Temujin was lucky enough to make his way back to his mother's camp without difficulty and must have been welcomed with great joy, the family's hardships increased after that. Because

Most of the land was arid steppe, and to keep alive in it at all a man needed a horse, weapons, flocks, and the company of his clansmen.

—R. P. LISTER
historian, on the land of the Mongols

they were too close to Targutai to be safe, the clan moved into the mountains, where they could find little to eat besides juniper berries, pine fruit, and rodents such as marmots and steppe rats. The number of their cattle and other beasts was dwindling, and only nine horses were left.

One day disaster struck. Without warning, a band of raiders from the steppe drew up in front of the tent, where all but one of the family's horses were grazing. The robbers drove the animals away over a hill before anyone could take up bows and arrows. The only horse left was one that Belgutai had taken that morning to hunt marmots. Everyone waited helplessly until Belgutai finally returned at sunset, leading the horse, which was laden with the rodents.

Both Belgutai and Kasar wanted to ride after the thieves, but Temujin decided to go alone. He stuffed a wad of dried meat under the horse's saddle and sped away across the rolling steppe. He tracked the men for three days and nights; on the fourth day, when his steed was stumbling with fatigue, he came upon a high plain where a youth of about his age was milking the mares in a large herd of horses.

The young man introduced himself as Bogurchi, the only son of Nakhu Bayan, and after hearing about Temujin's troubles he immediately offered his friendship and assistance. He tied Temujin's tired brown horse to one in his father's herd, gave the youth food and drink and a fresh mount, and announced that he would accompany him on the hunt. Leaving the full leather pails of milk in the middle of the pasture and taking care not to be seen from his father's tent, Bogurchi chose a fast cream-colored horse for himself and jumped into the saddle. Even as a youth Genghis Khan attracted followers easily.

The high-spirited pair searched the steppes for three days and became close friends. When Bogurchi learned who his companion was, he told Temujin that stories of his dramatic escape from Targutai were being told across the steppes and that his courage and resourcefulness were admired by many.

AP/WIDE WORLD PHOTOS

Mustang ponies are caught with a traditional pole lasso. Temujin and his first follower, Bogurchi, fearlessly tracked down thieves who had stolen the family's few horses.

Finally, near sundown at the end of the third day, they saw the eight stolen horses grazing near a small camp. Together Temujin and Bogurchi rounded up the eight animals and galloped away, pursued by the thieves. One man in the front of the stream of riders was preparing to use his lasso to pull one of the boys to the ground. Although Bogurchi wanted to use his bow against their enemies, Temujin did not want to risk or bring trouble to the Nakhu Bayan clan. Temujin took aim, and his pursuer stopped and readied his lasso. Darkness was falling quickly, however, and the other horsemen began to turn around. The rider who was threatening Temujin finally gave up, as well.

Temujin and Bogurchi rode all that night, stopping only to rest their horses, until they reached Bogurchi's tent. Temujin thanked his new friend heartily for his help. "I never could have done this alone," he said. "We shall share the horses; how many do you want?"

Bogurchi explained that he had ridden with Temujin as a friend and wanted no part of his property. "My father is called Nakhu the Rich," he added, "and everything he has will come to me. It is enough.

Followers present tributes to Genghis Khan, leader of all the Mongols. Even during his adolescence he was able to command respect.

I will accept nothing. What kind of service would it be if I were paid for it?"

The two youths swore eternal friendship and proceeded to Nakhu's tent. Bogurchi's father was mourning the disappearance of his son. When he saw that the boy was safe he wept harder, but now with tears of happiness. After scolding his son for the worry he had caused, he gave his approval to the friendship and urged the two to let no angry word ever come between them. Temujin had just acquired his first vassal, one who would serve him always.

The time had come to marry, and Temujin went to Dai Sechen to claim what was his, the lovely young Bortei, now a "fine-cheeked" girl with a dazzling face. The old chieftain welcomed Temujin warmly and after the marriage ceremony presented him with a magnificent coat of rare black sable — a small fortune that the young man quickly put to shrewd diplomatic use. Once Temujin had taken his ride back to his camp and seen that Bortei was settled in under Hoelun's care and guidance, he took the fur and rode away to the Black Forest area, on the western limits of the Mongol lands.

He stopped at the camp that belonged to Togrul, his father's sworn blood brother, or *anda*, and chief of the nomadic Keraits. Temujin presented the old man with the fabulous coat, explaining that because Togrul and Yesugei had been brothers by oath, Togrul now was like his own father. A solemn pact was struck: Togrul promised to help Temujin gather the people who had left him years before.

News of the agreement spread, and Temujin's following began to multiply. A man who had served under Yesugei the Brave came to the camp to ask Temujin to take his son, Jelmi, as his squire. When word got around that Temujin was accepting retainers (people in his service), young Mongols flocked to his camp to serve under the banner Hoelun had so proudly and desperately raised when the family was abandoned on the steppe.

Now Temujin had a wife, a mother urging revenge, a vassal, a squire, a powerful ally, four hardy brothers, and a modest number of horses and other animals. He also had the ability to defend what was his, to move quickly, to act decisively and at exactly the right time. Throughout the difficult years in his later youth, the young Genghis Khan had responded to each obstacle and setback by confronting it, adapting to it, learning from it. All the while, the power of his remarkable personality had been developing. Young though the future conqueror was in the days of his youthful exploits, he already had what one writer has called "the soul of a chief," commanding the respect of all who came in contact with him.

Temujin's courage and fairness, his regard for old friends, and his ferocity toward his enemies began to be discussed around campfires across the steppes. By the time Temujin was 17, the boy who had struggled for years to keep his helpless family alive in a brutal land had become a minor lord. The march to glory had begun.

In return for this gift, I will reunite your scattered people. . . . I will bring back to you your straying kinsmen.

—TOGRUL
Kerait chief, after receiving a sable coat from Temujin

3

The "Temporary" Khan

Be of one mind and one faith, that you may conquer your enemies and lead long and happy lives.
—GENGHIS KHAN
to his followers

Temujin's camp was still shrouded in darkness as he slept beside the beautiful Bortei, but the early-morning sky was beginning to flow with streaks of ghostly light. The camp was still except for a barely perceptible vibration. Hoelun's faithful old servant awoke, however, and put her ear to the ground. Then she screamed. "Hurry! Hurry!" she shouted. "The ground shakes with the sound of approaching horses."

The enemy swept in like a violent winter storm. They were Merkits from the south, who had not forgotten that Temujin's father had stolen the lady Hoelun from her Merkit bridegroom some 20 years before. Now the tribe would have its revenge: they would steal every woman in Temujin's camp — including his beloved Bortei. Just before their arrival, however, the stooped old servant who had heard the hoofbeats had led Bortei to a covered wooden wagon. Then she harnessed an ox and drove the cart up the banks of a nearby stream.

Temujin accepted his fate. Although his power and influence were growing, he still had only nine horses. He helped his mother and his 13-year-old sister, Temulin, mount; then he leaped on one horse, and the remainder were taken by his brothers, Kasar, Khaji'un, Temuga, and Belgutai, and his followers, Bogurchi and Jelmi. The group galloped

Statue of torch-bearing Mongol youth. After several tribes decided to unite under a single, strong leader, Temujin became Genghis Khan in 1183, when he was 21 years old.

MUSEUM OF FINE ARTS, BOSTON

AP/WIDE WORLD PHOTOS

Three generations of Mongol women wear traditional headdresses. Attacked by his mother's vengeful Merkit tribe, Temujin allowed his wife to be captured so that the rest of his family could escape.

away in the dawn, leaving Bortei and the woman servant behind.

According to Mongol legend, no fuss was made about abandoning Bortei. Temujin had no choice and didn't waste time lamenting what had to be done. Bortei didn't protest; just as the bride Hoelun had urged her own husband to leave her in order to save his life when Yesugei and his brothers overpowered them, Bortei, too, understood that, as one historian has written, "a man could soon find a wife somewhere else, but it took a long time to make a man."

Temujin's departure seems shocking from a 20th-century perspective, but the decision made perfect sense at the time. Grievances and reprisals, carried on for generations, were commonplace among the Mongols, and Temujin understood that Bortei was the first object of the Merkit raid. Had he sent her off on a horse and bravely stood his ground against the horsemen, he would surely have been killed, leaving his clan without any real protection. By leaving Bortei behind to be captured unarmed, Temujin not only helped ensure the escape of his family and followers but also gained the valuable getaway time.

The Merkit warriors caught Bortei and the servant, of course, but by then Temujin and his tribe had escaped to a dense forest at the foot of the mountain called Burkan Kaldun. The fugitives hid for three days until they were sure they were safe; then Temujin gave thanks to the Eternal Blue Heaven. Today, the national games of Mongolia, the *nadom*, are held every year to commemorate Temujin's escape.

Having protected most of his tribe, Temujin now was determined to find his wife. He took his brothers Kasar and Belgutai and rode to the land of the Black Forest, where Togrul lived. The time had come to take advantage of the alliance that had been sealed with the sable coat.

"I have not forgotten the help given to me by your father, Yesugei, who was my sworn brother," said Togrul. "And did I not promise to help you gather your people the day you brought me the black fur? I shall return Bortei to you if I have to destroy all the Merkits to do it!"

The half of my breast has been snatched from me. Shall we not avenge this injury?

—TEMUJIN
from a message requesting Jamuga's help in rescuing Bortei

The Merkits have cast me into affliction. They have carried off my wife.

—TEMUJIN
after Bortei's abduction

Before engaging in war on the fierce Merkits — a group of Mongol tribes who inhabited portions of two steppes as well as the Orhon and Selenga river region — Togrul enlisted the aid of another chieftain, Jamuga Sechen, who had been a boyhood friend of Temujin. Togrul and Jamuga each brought two *tumans* (regiments) of 2,500 men, and Temujin was able to mobilize a tuman of his own to join them. These were not the men trained only for war that Genghis Khan would assemble years later; they were ordinary herdsmen who responded to Temujin's call for aid, partly because they hoped that by joining him in a full-fledged foray with two other chieftains against the Merkits, they would acquire loot, animals, and women. They also knew that afterward they would be associated with a chieftain with real riches and power. Temujin's tuman was not large, but it was the first under his command. Although the Merkit clansmen fled along the Selenga River, in the northwest section of modern-day Mongolia, their pursuers caught up with them and killed all of the men who had stormed Temujin's sleeping camp. Temujin found Bortei in the enemy camp and discovered she was nine months pregnant. To complete their revenge, the Merkits had given Bortei to the youngest brother of the man who had first married Hoelun. As soon as Bortei returned to Temujin's tent, she gave birth to a boy her husband named Juchi, "the unexpected."

Being joined in battle against the Merkits had renewed the bonds between Temujin and Jamuga, who as children had sworn to be brothers by oath, but now were truly linked in spirit. They exchanged gold belts they had taken from the Merkits and then feasted, danced, and even slept under the same blanket at night. The goodwill lasted for 18 months; during this time the two camps were united and moved together to new grazing grounds.

The two young men had much in common. Both were shrewd and highly ambitious; each was courageous and adventure loving, and a natural leader of men. As time went by, however, the differences between them became clear. Most of Temujin's followers owned horses and cattle, whereas Jamuga's

AP/WIDE WORLD PHOTOS

Demonstrating legendary Mongol horsemanship, these children compete in a race near Ulan Bator. The national games of contemporary Mongolia, the *nadom*, are held each year in honor of Genghis Khan.

AP/WIDE WORLD PHOTOS

A 20th-century Mongol shepherd and his flock. The regiments of Genghis Khan and his early allies were not originally trained as warriors. Most were ordinary herdsmen who were easily attracted to a strong leader such as Genghis.

people owned sheep — a seemingly small matter today but meaningful to the Mongols. Temujin was of higher birth than his friend, who seemed to favor the common man and was accused of paying too little respect to tribal leaders. Temujin, on the other hand, courted the aristocracy, believing that therein lay the way to power and prestige. Friction was inevitable, and Hoelun and Bortei did all they could to separate the two sworn brothers. Undoubtedly they were jealous of Temujin's devotion to Jamuga.

Finally, in early summer, the breakup happened. The two chieftains had been leading a long, winding line of men, women, children, wagons, and animals to new pastures. Although they had been riding for only half a day, Jamuga apparently wanted to camp in the grassy river valley they had just come upon. Temujin wanted to continue, however, and Hoelun and Bortei urged him to do so regardless of Jamuga's reaction. Although Jamuga refused to continue, Temujin pushed ahead, realizing that each chieftain in the combined camp now had to decide whether or not to follow him. Temujin did not turn around for many hours. Finally, he stopped at the top of a hill to see how many people had come along. Groups of clansmen were streaming across the valley (including many families from Jamuga's camp), a testament to his personal magnetism and the talent for leadership that he had demonstrated in the last year and a half. Important Mongol princes brought wagons and animals with them; as the days passed, more people joined the procession.

Temujin had somehow chosen precisely the right moment to set out on his own; now he was the most powerful of all Mongol lords. He was also shrewd enough to negotiate with the greedy chieftains when necessary. Said one chief who had left Jamuga's camp: "If you want to be ruler of the people, as your actions suggest, what will be in it for me?"

Temujin replied, "Should I become such a one, I will put you in charge of 10,000 men."

But the crafty chief wanted more. "If you give me 100,000 to rule," he said, "let me also have 30 lovely girls to be my wives."

Temujin agreed and struck similar bargains with which other leaders were well pleased.

As summer wore on, the chieftains agreed to move the flocks and herds farther up in the mountains, and when they were settled, they conferred without Temujin. All agreed that a single leader was needed and that none of them could serve under any of the others. Yet no one objected to serving Temujin. His aristocratic background (his father having been a chieftain) marked him as a man of breeding, and his courage and resourcefulness already were legendary.

And so it was that a great tribal council was called in 1183. At this council the chiefs decided to name Temujin their khan, or ruler, with the title of Genghis — a word that carried the idea of strength

Do not break faith; do not untie this knot; do not once again rip off the collar of your coats.

—TOGRUL
Kerait chief, to the Mongols after Temujin was proclaimed khan

and fortitude and that may have had a religious meaning, as well. The leaders promised Genghis that he would ride at the head of the people against their enemies, and they swore that they would throw themselves "like lightning" upon his foes. They pledged to bring him their finest women and girls and high-stepping horses. Also, they promised to be obedient in war and never to meddle in his affairs in peacetime.

The chieftains should have paid attention to the intensity with which Genghis Khan began to organize his followers. "You who have stayed beside me from the first shall be above all others," he said. He appointed four loyal youths to be his personal guard and ordered them to arm themselves with bows and arrows. Three others who were devoted to him were put in charge of food and drink; another was made the commanding officer of the camp; still others were to watch over the slaves and servants, to be messengers, and to train the horses and protect the herds. The young Genghis Khan would flatter these intensely loyal men and give them lavish gifts, but he would be unremittingly cruel to any who would break his trust. Although years would

Vestiges of the violent way of life that challenged Genghis Khan and his followers continue to exist in modern-day Mongolia. Fleeing from bandits, these refugees cross the plains of Mongolia in 1935.

AP/WIDE WORLD PHOTOS

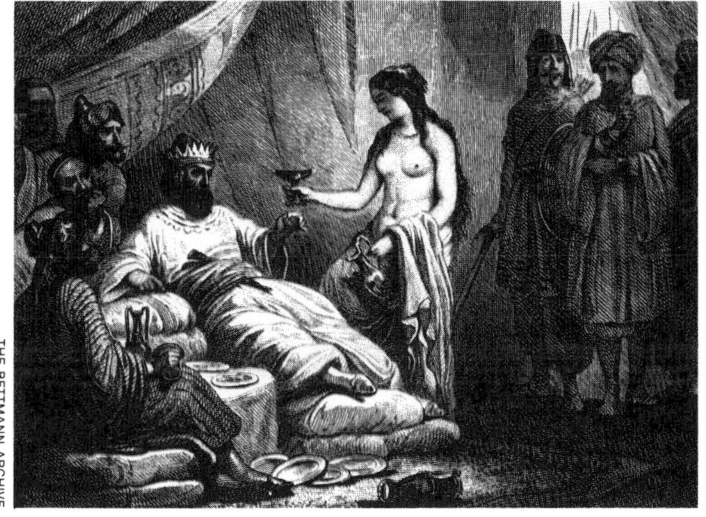
THE BETTMANN ARCHIVE

A serving woman offers a drink to Genghis Khan. The tribal chiefs who made him khan promised Genghis loyalty, obedience, and beautiful women.

pass before he would unite all the Mongol peoples, the young Genghis Khan was more powerful than ever.

After being named khan, Genghis sent two messengers to Togrul, the powerful Kerait chieftain who was also his friend and neighbor. It was important to have the Kerait's allegiance. Fortunately, the old ruler was pleased and told Genghis's representatives to be faithful to their leader.

Two other messengers took the news to Jamuga, who urged loyalty to the new khan but asked angrily, "Why didn't you name Temujin khan when he and I rode together? What is your reason for doing so now?"

In spite of their broken friendship, at this point neither Genghis nor Jamuga wanted to do harm to the other; hatred between the two was still to come.

4

The Master of Mongolia

> ***I will rule them by fixed laws [so] that rest and happiness shall prevail in the world.***
> —GENGHIS KHAN
> after being named khan

The moonlight was dimmed from time to time by drifting clouds as Jochi Darmala, from the camp of Genghis Khan, lay close to his galloping horse's back and headed for Jamuga's tents. That afternoon Jamuga's younger brother, Taichar, had decided that Jochi's horses were grazing on his grounds, and he had driven all of them into his own camp. Now Jochi intended to have the horses back — and to have his revenge.

He pressed himself still closer against his mount so that he would be the smallest possible target when he shot his arrows. He rode around the edges of the circle of tents, shouting again and again at the men rushing from their tents. One arrow lodged in Taichar's spine and killed him instantly. When Jochi's quiver was completely empty, he sped back home. Jamuga was furious. He had helped Genghis rescue Bortei from the Merkit, and in return his old friend had left him, had lured important men from his camp, had been declared khan . . . and now this. Jamuga gathered an army together and rode to Genghis's camp. Ill prepared for the attack, Genghis Khan was routed and many of his

A Mongol man carries the traditional bow and quiver of arrows. The bow was the most potent weapon of Genghis Khan's armies. His swift mounted archers decimated less mobile foes with showers of armor-piercing arrows.

AP/WIDE WORLD PHOTOS

Genghis devised strategies of organization and defense unique among the Mongols of his time. Some consider him the most brilliant military genius in history.

followers were killed or captured. When Jamuga was back in his own camp again, he ordered his people to fill immense cauldrons with water and to light fires underneath. As soon as the water bubbled and steamed, 70 captured chieftains were boiled alive. When all of the men were dead, Jamuga cut off the most powerful chieftain's head and rode again to Genghis's camp, dragging it behind his horse.

Although some legends have it that Genghis himself was responsible for many such horrible deeds, the truth is that as a rule he was not pointlessly cruel. While he was ruthless with anyone who betrayed him or brought harm to his family and followers, he did not delight in torturing a condemned man.

The outrageous act of vengeance may have helped Jamuga vent his rage, but it had another effect the chieftain did not anticipate: two large clans, the Uru'uts and the Mangquts, left to join Genghis's side because of their horror at what had happened. It was not long before Genghis had regrouped his forces.

At about this time, in 1198, Genghis sent one of his speedy "arrow messengers" to Togrul. Genghis proposed that his clan unite with Togrul's to fight on behalf of the northern Chinese rulers; the Qin had invited the Mongols to help them fend off tribes of fierce Tatars, old enemies of the Mongols. Togrul accepted Genghis's proposal, and together the two leaders crushed the Tatar forces. The Qin richly rewarded the Mongols for this assistance.

Many of the central Asian tribes had begun to fear Genghis Khan's growing power. In 1201 a number of chieftains formed an alliance against him. They elected Jamuga as their leader. One of Jamuga's first moves was to attack Genghis's forces. But even though Jamuga had a much larger army, Genghis's men were far better disciplined and defeated the aggressors easily.

Genghis Khan had organized his men in a way that was unique among the Mongols at that time. He formed a mounted cavalry by dividing his warriors into squads of 10, with 10 squads in a squadron and 10 squadrons in a *quran* of 1,000 men. Ten qurans together formed a tuman of 10,000 riders. At first, Genghis had approximately 13 qurans and held daily drills and practices to teach them to move as units. The men were able to respond to his orders immediately and to fight in hand-to-hand combat as a team. The very best warriors led the qurans, and they responded to Genghis with perfect obedience and demanded the same from their men.

Genghis Khan also devised a new defensive strategy. Instead of fighting from within a circle of wagons, Genghis ordered the cavalry to line up in front of heavily armed men who were positioned in a long line in front of a dense forest. The qurans were arranged in blocs that were 100-men wide and 10-men deep. The women and children were far off to one side, safe within a circle of wagons. As the attackers advanced, the men on horseback would let fly a blizzard of arrows and then would hasten to the rear. The heavily armed units would then charge and rapidly overcome the enemy. This highly disciplined army was a weapon that Genghis Khan would use to conquer much of the world.

BETTMANN ARCHIVE

This 14th-century Mongol helmet is similar to those worn by Genghis Khan's heavy cavalry regiments. The Mongols also wore complete body armor of leather reinforced with metal.

After defeating Jamuga's forces, Genghis Khan overcame all the hostile Mongol and Tatar tribes in eastern Mongolia, sometimes killing all the men, capturing the women, and bringing the children into his own tribe. Jamuga escaped to western Mongolia, leaving Genghis supreme in the east.

Plotting and scheming against Genghis Khan continued, of course. Even his aging ally Togrul was persuaded with lies by Sengun, his envious eldest son, to side with Jamuga and to lead an army of Keraits against the son of Yesugei the Brave. When Genghis Khan learned about the invasion from an informer, he hurriedly prepared for battle and marched west into central Mongolia. The bloody, exhausting Battle of Khalakhaljit lasted for several days, with neither side clearly the victor. Finally, in the protection of darkness, Genghis decided to retreat to eastern Mongolia, where his horses could graze and his men could fortify themselves with fish and game. Togrul, Jamuga, and Sengun returned with their followers to the central region.

Genghis then sent two messengers to Togrul and

Jamuga, bearing carefully worded calls for peace. He reminded the old Kerait chieftain of the days when he and his own father, Yesugei, had been blood brothers; that he, Genghis, had chosen Togrul to be his adopted father; that he had fought for Togrul and assisted him.

In his message to Jamuga, Genghis spoke to his former anda of the bitterness and envy that led Jamuga to conspire against him. The messengers returned to Genghis with a reply that the battle would continue.

As Genghis withdrew even farther, most of his warriors remained with him in the crisis, despite the fact that Mongols usually deserted leaders who were not victorious. Later, Genghis would reward all the men who remained loyal with great wealth and special privileges, such as permission to enter his tent freely and immunity from punishment for as many as nine serious crimes.

In the next months, the alliance between Jamuga's and Togrul's peoples broke down, and many

This miniature illustrates a stand-off between the defenders of a walled city and Mongol troops brandishing the severed head of a defeated enemy. The Mongol nomads initially had trouble conquering fortified cities.

THE BETTMANN ARCHIVE

CULVER PICTURES

Genghis remained a nomad all his life and used a tent for his palace. No one was permitted to pitch a tent before the khan's was erected, and care was taken that his view was kept uninterrupted clear to the horizon.

Keraits grew restive under Togrul's rule. When a Kerait chieftain left the camp and told Genghis about all the dissension, the shrewd Mongol leader decided it was time to respond to his enemies' betrayal and trickery with treachery of his own. His brother Kasar, who had been in Togrul's camp when hostilities broke out, had managed to escape, but his family was still in the enemy camp. Genghis now asked Kasar to send a cunning message to the old chief saying that he had searched for Genghis but couldn't find him anywhere and that since his brother surely was dead, he now wanted to rejoin Togrul's camp. Togrul believed the story completely and ordered a huge feast to celebrate Genghis's death and the surrender of his enemy's brother.

As the festivities got under way, Genghis and his army were marching into central Mongolia. He took the Kerait forces completely by surprise and defeated them after three days of fierce combat in the Battle of Mount Jeje'er. Sengun and Togrul rode away to the west but were soon killed by hostile tribesmen. Jamuga hid with the Naiman. This powerful tribe spent several months a year in towns built centuries before by the Uighur, ironworkers and agriculturists who had developed a great civilization in the 8th century. The semisettled Naiman had inherited a great deal of the Uighur culture, including a written language, and were well organized and

LITERARY FORM.

COLLOQUIAL FORM.

BURIAT COLLOQUIAL FORM.

CULVER PICTURES

Samples of Mongolian script. Although illiterate, Genghis grasped the significance written symbols held for the future of his people. He insisted that his children be taught to read and write.

relatively civilized; they considered the Mongols illiterate savages.

When Jamuga, who was determined to establish alliances with the partly settled peoples as well as with the nomads of the steppe, warned the Naiman and the forest-dwelling Merkits that Genghis Khan posed a terrible threat, they believed him and began preparing for battle. Thanks to the reporting of certain spies in the Naiman territory, however, Genghis learned of the war plans and called a council of his chieftains to tell them of the danger and to ask for their support. The majority voted to help him, and Genghis rode westward with an army of some 80,000 men.

The cruel Naiman king, Tayan — who had been responsible for Togrul's death and in fact put the chief's head on display — was joined by Jamuga, the Merkits, and some Tatars. In 1204 Tayan assembled his army and waited at a place called Chakirma'ut for his enemy to approach. Genghis Khan's warriors were in battle formation when they met the Naiman and overpowered them with their flanking movements, counterattacks, and shrewd tactics. Jamuga and his followers retreated when their defeat became apparent. Many of the Merkit fled, the Naiman army began to disintegrate, and Genghis's forces overran them all.

THE BETTMANN ARCHIVE

Mongol arms and armor. Although armor offered Genghis's warriors some protection against arrows, their chief advantages over the enemy were the mobility afforded by their excellent horsemanship and their ability to make tightly coordinated maneuvers.

At this point the Mongol showed uncharacteristic lenience. He ordered his army to refrain from plundering the Naiman's possessions, and he spared the lives of the chieftains who were taken prisoner. He returned their weapons and their horses and asked them to serve him with the same devotion they had shown to their former lords. The brilliant leader understood the importance of expanding his rule: with the vanquished Naiman behind him now, he was the undisputed leader of more than 2 million people, the lord of all the land from Siberia to the Great Wall of China. He made the Merkit beauty Kulan one of his wives; in this way he had his revenge for the capture of Bortei years before and he gained a companion in many future campaigns — a woman whose loveliness has been immortalized in Mongol poetry.

Not long after the battle ended, Genghis's retainers brought a prisoner before him, a man dressed in fine clothes and carrying something Genghis had never seen. The man proudly explained that he was Tatatungo, a Uighur who had served the Naiman chief Tayan, and that he was bearing Tayan's seal. He showed Genghis the symbols engraved upon it, and Temujin, whose people had never had a written language, immediately grasped the significance of such symbols. He made Tatatungo his official scribe and ordered him to teach all the khan's children and the children of his chief nobles how to decipher

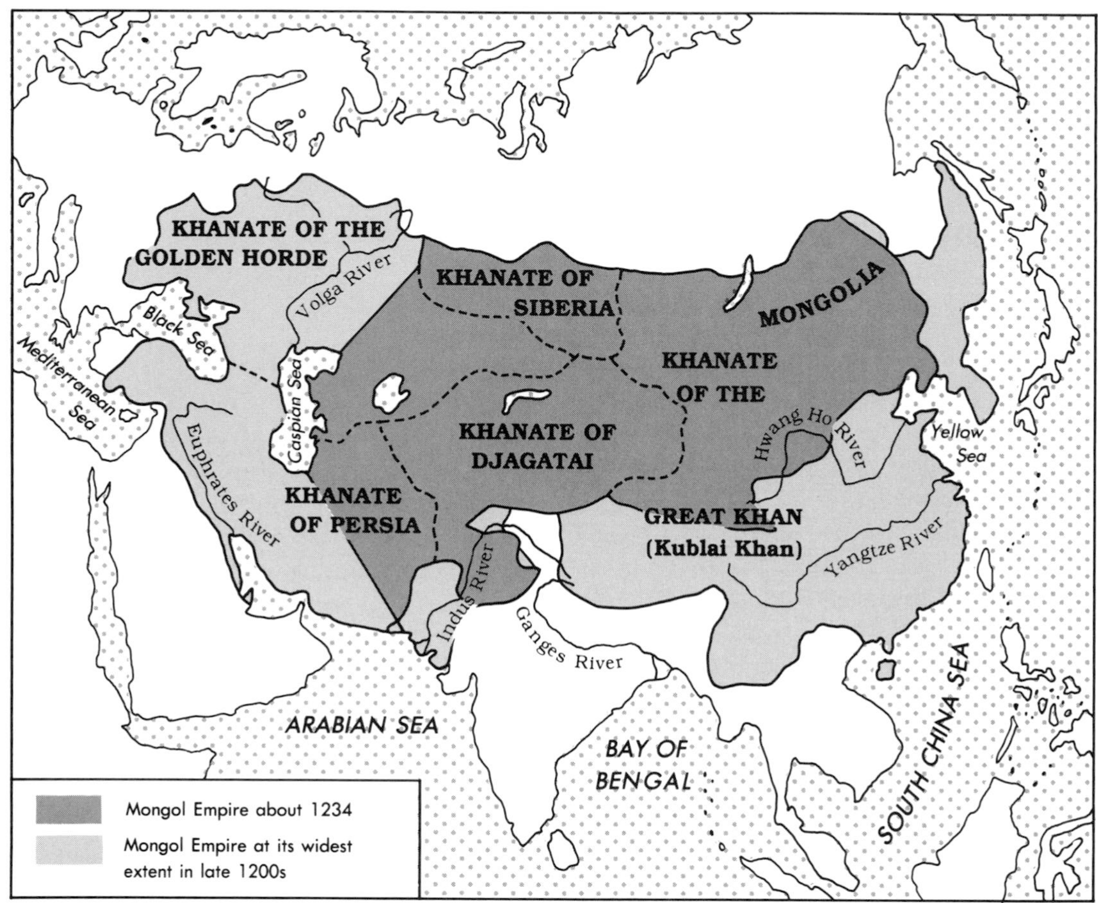

Map depicting the Mongol empire in the 13th century. The darker areas show the empire's extent seven years after Genghis Khan's death; the lighter areas represent additional conquests made by his heirs.

the symbols and how to use them to communicate.

For a time after the Battle of Chakirma'ut, Jamuga and his followers managed to hide from Genghis's warriors, who were sent to subjugate any remaining resisters. But Jamuga's clansmen finally decided to save themselves by turning their leader over to Genghis. The Mongol, who could under no circumstances tolerate disloyalty, promptly ordered that everyone in the clan, down to the smallest child, be killed. A people who betrayed their own leader would be forever untrustworthy, he believed. He spared his former sworn brother, however, and tried to make peace with him.

Jamuga, however, spoke to him with wisdom. "When we were blood brothers long ago," he said sadly, "we rode together and ate together and spoke to one another in ways we will always remember. But then certain people set us against one another, and I feel shame when I remember the words I spoke against you. Today I cannot be your comrade, for I would always cause you to be uneasy by day and to sleep poorly at night. You have surpassed me. Now let me die quickly, without the shedding of my blood, so that I can protect your descendants forever."

Genghis was sorrowful when he heard Jamuga's words, and he said, "Jamuga has always gone his own way. He now wants his life to end. Let it be done." He ordered that Jamuga be crushed to death in such a way that no blood was spilled, for the Mongols believed that the blood contains the soul. Jamuga was then buried with great ceremony in a high place, from which his spirit could forever watch over the steppe.

For the first time in history, one man commanded the diverse bands of Mongol nomads who until now had been constantly warring. They respected and honored their leader, who gave them a sense of intense pride in themselves as Mongols. These fierce and independent people were stirred by a heady sense of nationalism, a realization that they were an important nation, not just a temporary alliance of tribes.

Genghis Khan dominated the vast area that today is known as Outer Mongolia. To the south was the Tangut state, Hsi Hsia; to the east was the Qin Empire that lay behind the Great Wall; to the west stretched Kara Khitai, an enormous kingdom southwest of Mongolia. At one time the ancient empire of China had encompassed these realms, but its rulers gradually weakened until, 300 years before Genghis's time, the kingdom had come apart. Little did the proud princes of the lands realize that a revolution had taken place among the much-reviled barbarian nomads — or what shocking changes lay ahead.

CULVER PICTURES

Genghis Khan transformed bands of loosely allied tribes into a mighty empire. Respect and honor for their warrior khan bred pride in the unified Mongol people.

Clara Nargeot del.
Nargeot Sc

5

Order on the Steppes

> ***Heaven has appointed me to rule all the nations, for hitherto there has been no order upon the steppes.***
> —GENGHIS KHAN

The 400,000 felt tents in Genghis Khan's camp stretched for miles, and above the grassy plains rose a joyous medley of singing, shouting, storytelling, and boasting about heroic deeds both past and to come. Musicians played and people danced and sang under the open sky. Wooden carts holding steaming vats of cooked horsemeat in a fiery sauce moved slowly through the throngs. The Mongols gorged themselves and slaked the violent thirst that came from the spicy food with gulps of a powerful fermented drink made from mare's milk.

An hour before, Genghis had been in his tent awaiting word from the tribal council, to which all the nobles in the land had been summoned. A huge canopy shaded the front of his tent, and the wooden poles supporting the richly embroidered cloth were decorated with hammered metal. Another sign of his status was the long lance positioned at one side of the entrance; to it were attached nine white yak-tails, signifying the nine courageous generals who were his chief commanders.

No structures were permitted to block the view from Genghis's tent — yet his relatives, chieftains, and military commanders had done just that as they streamed into the open space and called for him with mighty shouts.

The wisdom, determination, and military cunning of Genghis Khan earned him absolute power over a huge, sprawling empire. His decisions often reflected a profound knowledge of human nature.

THE BETTMANN ARCHIVE

THE BETTMANN ARCHIVE

Genghis Khan is inaugurated as the first true ruler of all the Mongol tribes. Shortly after this ceremony Genghis created the *yasak*, a revolutionary new code of laws and behavior.

When Genghis appeared, the people declared that they would obey his commands. Genghis had replied, "From now on, my word shall be my sword."

Several nobles spread a thick felt blanket on the ground at Genghis's feet and asked him to sit in the center. When he had done so, they lifted the cloth by its corners and carried their khan to a throne. The chieftains and nobles — the rulers Genghis now ruled — went down to their knees and bowed to him; then six of them lifted the throne and carried him through the kneeling crowd.

A great festival began, and the people reveled in their leader's happiness and strength, rejoicing, too, in their own good fortune. The celebration would continue for weeks.

The year was 1206; Genghis Khan was 44 years old, and one of the major events in world history had just taken place. Genghis was the first man to rule over all of the Mongols — thanks to his wisdom, the force of his personality, his military acumen, and his fierce determination to accomplish every undertaking. True, Genghis had been named khan 23 years earlier, at the time he and Jamuga had parted, but he was not given absolute power then;

he was simply declared the leader of a group of tribes. Now, however, his kingdom stretched for a thousand miles, from the peaks of the Altai in the west to the summits of the Khingan in the east; from the shining waters of Lake Baikal in the northern region all the way to the shimmering sands of the Gobi Desert, 600 miles to the south. More than 2 million people were united behind him now, ready to respond to his slightest command. Even the most ordinary nomad considered himself elevated simply by virtue of being a subject of Genghis Khan. From the time Genghis was proclaimed khan, all the nomads in the land, regardless of tribe and origin, called themselves Mongols.

As the festivities continued, Genghis began to reorganize his nation. Many of his decisions reflected an amazing understanding of human nature — so much so, in fact, that Genghis never had any reason to regret any of his choices. The men he assigned to various positions performed honorably and well.

Genghis's generals were astonished by many of their ruler's choices for important posts but never more so than by his appointment of one of the bravest and strongest chieftains to a position that involved no leadership whatsoever.

"You are correct," said Genghis when the men told him that they thought the warrior had been misassigned. "This man is indeed a hero and an able fighter. And it's true that he scoffs at hardship and ignores fatigue. But precisely because he assumes that every man who serves under him is like himself, he should not be in command of an army. A good commander," he went on, "must understand what his followers feel — or he will allow his warriors to suffer and his horses to starve."

One of the most important decisions Genghis made in the first days of his rule as the khan of khans was to instruct Tatatungo, the literate Uighur, to stay at his side and record his words. "I shall draw up a yasak [a code of laws]," Genghis said, "which shall guide all men who come after me, even for a thousand years. If they depart from my yasak, the realm will crumble. They will then call for Genghis Khan but will not find him."

He quenched his thirst with his own spittle and chewed his own gums for supper. He exerted himself till the sweat of his brow moistened the soles of his feet.

—anonymous contemporary, on Genghis Khan

Those who were adept and brave fellows I have made military commanders. Those who were quick and nimble I have made herders of horses. Those who were not adept I have given a small whip and sent to be shepherds.

—GENGHIS KHAN
on the reorganization
of his followers

The yasak included laws prohibiting lying, spying, quarreling, getting involved in the disagreements of others, using magic (since great harm could be done if the wrong person took advantage of the superstitions of others), and interfering with another's actions. Many codes of behavior pertained to the army and to prisoners; others delineated the obligations of women — for example, that they must perform all their husbands' duties when their mates were away at war.

Death was a common punishment for certain violations involving the nomads' well-being, such as the failure of a soldier during battle to pick up a bow or quiver that a fellow warrior ahead of him had dropped, and urinating on water — a particularly important hygienic consideration in parts of Mongolia where water was scarce. Robbing a nomad of one or more of his animals was another capital crime, since Genghis knew from experience what the loss of an animal meant to a poor wanderer.

Genghis appointed a permanent general staff to assign winter and summer pastures to various tribes according to their needs, to decide how many men must go to war when campaigns began, to report on the situation in bordering countries, to arbitrate disputes, to guarantee safety on roads, and even to return lost animals to their owners. Characteristically, the khan of khans remembered those who had been loyal to him. He thus gave a supreme position to Bogurchi, who as a youth had ridden with him in pursuit of eight stolen horses. "My Bogurchi," said Genghis, "my staunchest companion, you shall be the commander of all my armies, and you will watch over my empire."

As time went on, the ideal of honor became all-important among the Mongols, and theft, murder, violent robbery, and adultery disappeared altogether. One historian relates that all persons who were rightfully accused of a crime admitted what they had done; in some cases men who broke Genghis's laws turned themselves in and asked to be punished.

Genghis Khan's military system was as effective as his civil strategy. He kept a personal bodyguard of 1,000 men and a standing army of 10,000 nearby. He often called up vast numbers of men for training maneuvers, and sometimes summoned them for hunts, which actually amounted to war games. He kept the military system he had established earlier, with its ranking of units from 10-man squads to 10,000-man tumans. Sometimes divisions were organized into a horde of 30,000 or more — a terrifying weapon that Genghis Khan used brilliantly.

When armies were on the move, enough horses were brought along behind a division to provide each warrior with two or three extra mounts. That practice accounted for the Mongols' ability to advance for days at a time at speeds that were remarkable in comparison to their enemies' progress.

The Mongols were shrewd in their use of mares in battle: during the long days on the steppes, the milk provided ready refreshment. One drawback to the reliance on horses was that the soldiers sometimes had to adapt their military strategy to the availability of fodder; thus, Genghis Khan often

A 13th-century Japanese scroll depicts Mongols assembling for battle. When not engaged in wars of conquest, Genghis Khan's soldiers took part in training maneuvers and war games patterned after hunting expeditions.

THE BETTMANN ARCHIVE

Mongol women display wealth and social position with richly jeweled headdresses. Under rules laid down in Genghis Khan's yasak, women were given control of all family possessions. Their primary duty, however, was to enhance their husbands' reputations.

AP/WIDE WORLD PHOTOS

opted for winter campaigns, when the rugged horses not only could cross frozen rivers and streams quickly but also could find grass underneath the snow in an area that would be parched and yellow in summer.

The soldiers themselves were men from 15 to 70 years old. In times of peace, the commanders would, with the assistance of instructors, train the men and inspect their weapons. Each had to see to it that his people could respond instantly; if a commander failed in any respect, he could be demoted to ordinary soldier. At the same time, warriors who performed with distinction would be promoted to ever-higher positions.

Some two-thirds of the soldiers carried the huge Mongol bow and a generous supply of arrows, a lasso or a collection of light spears, and a sword. They were protected only by leather shields, helmets, and sometimes leather tunics (long jackets). Heavy cavalrymen, on the other hand, wore full leather armor and carried a lance, a scimitar (a saber with a huge curved blade), and often bows and arrows. All the men wore coarse silk shirts next to their skin, for Genghis had discovered that arrows seldom pierced the sturdy natural fiber. Wounded Mongol soldiers were never abandoned, and assistance was given as quickly as possible.

According to one military historian, until recent times no soldiers have been as mobile as Genghis Khan's troops. As a result of intensive practice drilling, the men were so skilled that they could respond to any command instantly and accurately — and as a smoothly coordinated unit.

Genghis was well aware of the importance of taking and keeping the initiative in battle, and his warriors always attacked — even when they in fact were on the defensive. Ultimately, their deep and highly disciplined formations always broke up the enemy's less well-managed and thinner ranks.

At the beginning of a war, the Mongols moved forward on a remarkably broad front, keeping in touch with one another by means of the messenger service that Genghis Khan had developed when he became the supreme ruler. Jelmi, son of Togrul, the chieftain who had accepted the sable coat years before, was Genghis's second most important vassal, and he was put in charge of the arrow messengers. Everyone in the land, from the poorest herdsman to the noblest prince, had to move aside to let these remarkable horsemen pass. The men were wrapped in cloth bandages from head to toe to help protect them from the battering they took as they sped along for days, sleeping in the saddle instead of stopping along the way. When a horse became exhausted, a fresh one had to be provided by anyone who was nearby. Thus, the riders could cover in several days distances that took ordinary horsemen weeks to travel. In this way Genghis Khan was al-

THE BETTMANN ARCHIVE

This example of 13th-century Chinese Buddhist art depicts a many-armed deity. One of the ways in which Genghis Khan maintained his expanding empire was by tolerating religious diversity.

ways kept informed about events in the farthest reaches of his realm. During wartime the messengers were also used to take information from one commander to another.

Another innovation that was key to Genghis Khan's military success was the way he used the element of surprise. He seldom repeated patterns of movement in the same campaign. Sometimes his soldiers feigned retreat when actually they were mounting fresh horses that would outmaneuver and outrun the enemy's flagging steeds when the Mongols resumed their attack. At other times they would strike the enemy from behind. Often, however, Genghis's generals would send the light cavalry forward in columns spread out across an enormous front. If the enemy proved too strong, the light soldiers could retreat quickly — or Genghis Khan might use various diversions to engage the opposing forces while other Mongols advanced to the side and rear. Eventually, being far better trained than any other troops, the Mongol warriors would close in from all sides and overpower the enemy with an intense concentration of arrows and javelins.

The role of women in 13th-century Mongolia was highly specific and in one respect surprising. Unlike other Asiatic females, Mongol women had their husbands' trust and could do whatever they wished with the men's possessions — buy, sell, or trade. Every woman was obliged to obey her husband, however, and was expected to help build his reputation. As Genghis Khan put it, "Good men are recognized by the goodness of their wives." Adultery resulted in death.

Every man had to be in a constant state of readiness for war. The warrior was responsible for the maintenance of his weapons; his wife's duty was to make sure that his heavy sheepskin cloaks, felt socks, and leather boots were clean and ready to wear. In addition, she kept his saddlebags filled with strips of dried meat and milk curds; his leather pouch, with mare's milk.

In the next 50 years Genghis Khan's army would prove to be the deadliest military weapon yet created; that remarkable organization enabled the new Mongol Empire to maintain its expensive feudal structure in a poor pastoral society that produced very few goods and services. The princes and leaders needed to live in a style befitting their rank, with fancy embroidered clothes, costly ornaments in their tents, and finery for their wives and mistresses. The army required weapons and special clothes and equipment, as well.

Muslim traders who moved between central Asia and China, the empire behind the Great Wall, told Genghis Khan of the riches and wonders of the Qin Empire: of amazing roads that crossed over rivers, of enormous floating houses that moved upstream, of grand chairs fastened to poles that transported nobles through the streets, of walled-in towns so large that they could house the entire Mongol nation, of devices that could throw fire, of rockets that shattered with tremendous noise and broke everything around them into pieces, of carts of war that were pulled by 20 horses.

Genghis listened and marveled at the wonders of the land, and at the power of the emperor. Surely the empire represented a threat to his young kingdom; indeed, over the centuries the Qin had been skillful in encouraging one nomad tribe to turn against another, thus preventing any attempts at unification. Past khans with far less power than Genghis had been executed, poisoned, or killed in battle. To succeed in a fight against these advanced urban people — however internally divided China was, with two dynasties in the land and a peasant uprising raging in the north, and however weak its economy — Genghis knew that he needed to prepare himself and his people for the mighty struggle that lay ahead.

Because the Tangut state of Hsi Hsia, which lay to the south of Mongolia, was organized much like China, Genghis knew that to wage war there would give his men superb training. In 1207, the year after he became khakan, or the khan of khans, the 45-year-old Genghis invaded the state of the Tibetan race of Tanguts and won the first battle there. But then his legions of horsemen reached a tremendous

Perhaps my children will live in stone houses and walled towns — not I.

—GENGHIS KHAN

fortress called Volohai. The Mongols urged Genghis to attack, and he let them make the attempt. Those nomads who were not killed were quickly driven back. His men, unaccustomed to losing, began to be hesitant and afraid, and Genghis knew that to return home would be to shake the soldiers' faith in their khan. Genghis knew that he lacked the war machines that would enable him successfully to lay siege to the city. But in this crisis Genghis was, as always, amazingly resourceful and decided to outwit the enemy.

Mongol legend has it that before his army could be decimated, Genghis sent a messenger to the commander of Volohai saying that he would call off his men if the general would deliver to him a thousand cats and many thousands of swallows.

Somewhat surprisingly, the enemy leader complied with the bizarre demand and had the creatures delivered to the Mongols. Genghis instructed his men to tie bits of cloth to the cats' and swallows' tails and to set the makeshift wicks on fire. The birds and cats were then set free. In their pain and terror the birds flew into the city to seek their nests, while the cats ran to small crevices and holes between the stones of the city walls and reentered the city; all set hundreds of fires in their panic. In the midst of the confusion, Genghis and his men overran the fortified town and finally forced the enemy to make a guarded peace. The king of Hsi Hsia agreed to pay Genghis a yearly tribute of valuable animals and goods.

Genghis understood, however, as his men did not, that the army was powerless against fortresses. He could not rely on clever ruses alone; he had to find a way to apply the lessons of the siege to his battle tactics while his men were still longing for new conquests.

Genghis returned to Mongolia to confront the problem head-on. The first thing he did was send all his arrow messengers to summon every chieftain and general in his empire. He established a mighty war academy in which all the hard lessons of Volohai were to be analyzed. To daily cavalry drills and periodic war games he added courses in laying siege

AP/WIDE WORLD PHOTOS

A modern weaver works on a rug with an ancient Mongol design. Skilled craftsmen, scholars, and officials were prized as booty of war. Genghis made use of the artistic achievements of conquered societies in the new Mongol culture he helped create.

to walled cities. As a result, his warriors learned to make enormous ladders that permitted men to scale the walls of fortresses, and they prepared special equipment, such as oversized shields behind which many men would be protected from arrows and spears directed at them from a great height. When the courses were completed, the leaders returned to their people to assemble great trains of weaponry, shields, carts, and equipment and to continue to practice the art of siegecraft.

Finally, in 1209, two years after his first encounter with walled cities, Genghis Khan led 80,000 superbly trained warriors across the Gobi Desert, and decisively defeated the Hsi Hsia army of 50,000 that met them at the country's border. He then proceeded to Volohai, which had been entirely rebuilt, and easily overcame the enemy.

Next Genghis and his army advanced toward the Hsi Hsia's capital city on the banks of the Hwang Ho (also Yellow or Huang Ho) River. When he en-

Long caravans of camels carried supplies to advancing Mongol armies during campaigns of conquest. Careful structuring of supply lines enabled Genghis Khan's troops to strike quickly and carry out lengthy sieges.

countered an army of 120,000 men, he used a favorite ploy and pretended to retreat. The unsuspecting Hsi Hsia warriors gave chase and headed directly into an ambush.

When Genghis attacked the capital itself, however, he found it extremely well defended. For two long months he and his men tried to enter the city, but the extended siege seemed futile. Genghis had an inspiration: to divert the river away from the city and thus to deprive the enemy of its lifeline. Genghis's army lacked skilled engineers, however, and the dam that finally was built soon broke and flooded the Mongol camp, forcing the men to retreat to safe ground.

At this point Genghis sent Tangut prisoners of war to the emperor to tell him that if he paid a tribute to the khan of khans, the Mongols would return to their homeland. Genghis was aware that the lengthy battle had cut off the so-called Silk Road that passed from China through Hsi Hsia to Persia and that the economy of the country would be threatened if the war were to continue. The emperor was only too happy to end the hostilities and gave Genghis falcons, fine cloth, many rare white camels, and assurances of future military assistance. He even gave Genghis one of his beautiful daughters, evidence that he considered Genghis Khan to be a great ruler.

His army is as numerous as ants and locusts. His warriors are as brave as lions.

—anonymous contemporary description of Genghis's army

As Genghis was preparing to return with his thousands of soldiers to the steppes, one of his messengers reached him with the news that a group representing the Chinese emperor had crossed the Great Wall. When Genghis received the head of the delegation from the emperor of the decadent Qin Dynasty in northern China, the ambassador informed him that he had an important imperial message. He also told Genghis that the message was to be acknowledged with a *kowtow* — a demonstration of homage made by kneeling and touching one's forehead to the ground.

It is difficult to imagine the ruler of Mongolia and Hsi Hsia performing such an act of self-abasement — and rather easy to suppose that Genghis was outraged. Genghis had heard from one of his messengers about a new emperor named Wei Wang, but he pretended ignorance — the better to lay the groundwork for the insult he planned to deliver.

He politely asked the name of the new emperor; when Wei Wang was named, he turned to the south, as if to begin to kowtow, but instead of making obeisance, he spat with great force, saying that he was surprised that an idiot could become emperor. With that, he leaped on his horse and rode off.

When the delegate returned to the emperor's palace in Beijing with a somewhat watered down version of what the barbarian Mongol had said, the furious emperor ordered the messenger cast into prison for bringing such evil news. Wei Wang then sent a general with an enormous array of soldiers to march across the Gobi Desert into the barbarians' land to punish their uncouth leader; he sent another to supervise the building of a new fortress near the Great Wall in order to repel any Mongol invasion.

The general who had been ordered to go to Mongolia was not eager to die on the long march through the barbarians' territory, so he and his men simply plundered the camps of peaceful tribes on the other side of the Great Wall. But his restraint failed to keep him safe: when Genghis learned that Chinese troops were outside the wall, he sent several divisions of 30,000 or 40,000 warriors to attack. Wei Wang's men were defeated, and the partly built fortress was demolished. The emperor promptly lost his taste for confrontation, and throughout the next year Genghis Khan was never once disturbed in his preparations for a march across the civilized world.

Although it is easy to assume that Genghis, inflamed with power and the new spirit of Mongol nationalism, consciously set out to conquer the world, several important facts should be kept in mind. As mentioned earlier, the young nomad empire had many hierarchies of leaders of various ranks and degrees of prestige who now needed to show off their status by the clothes they wore, the kind of tents they lived in, the way their families dressed, and the number of possessions they had. In addition, the huge Mongol army required

China's Qin emperor, Wei Wang, sent troops to confront Genghis beyond the Great Wall. The Mongols promptly defeated this army, then prepared to subjugate all of China.

THE BETTMANN ARCHIVE

hundreds of thousands of weapons, none of which could be produced by the people.

China and other neighboring countries needed meat, furs, milk, and assorted products of the Mongol economy, but peaceful trade was out of the question. To the southeast of Mongolia was a China divided between the oppressive dynasties, or powerful ruling families, of the Qin in the north and the Song in the south. The country's economy was crumbling, and peasants in the north were fighting, their rebellion fueled by their rage, humiliation, and desperation at their poverty — and by the cunning encouragement of the Song. At the same time, the empire of the Kara Khitai peoples to the southwest of Mongolia and the Khwarezmian Empire in the west had disrupted China's ancient trade routes.

Thus, the Mongols would take what they needed from others by force, as did the most powerful tribes in the days of Yesugei the Brave. The difference was that now all the clans and tribes in central Asia were united behind a single powerful individual — who happened to be a military genius and a spellbinding leader.

It has been written that after he was made khan of khans, Genghis gazed at the vast sea of tents and spoke of his people with a feeling that seemed close to love. Genghis compared his warriors and archers to a "vast forest of many trees" and said that he wanted to "sweeten their mouths with the gift of sweet sugar . . . to give them to drink from pure and tasty rivers," and to provide their animals with fine grass.

The relentless and bloody march against a succession of empires was about to begin.

丁卯暮春
大好河山
高維嶽
大境門
紅錫包

6

The Mongol War Machine

> *They rode over vast tracts of the world, sacking cities and defeating the armies of their enemies, without caring much what the cities were called, or what king they were defeating.*
> —R. P. LISTER
> historian, on Genghis's armies

Genghis Khan's throbbing head felt as light as the clouds in the Great Blue Sky, home of the powerful spirits to whom he had been speaking for the past three days and nights. His eyelids stung; the walls of his tent seemed to waver: he had had but five hours' sleep in the last three days. His stomach burned as though it had been scraped raw: he had had nothing to eat or drink since more than 200,000 Mongol warriors had gathered at his camp on the Kerulen River, in central Mongolia, in answer to his summons. More than three days before he had announced to the multitude that hundreds of years of persecution of the nomads were about to be avenged with war upon the Qin Empire behind the Great Wall. As his words were repeated over and over again until every person in the great throng had received the news, great waves of joyous shouting burst forth. The Mongols' great and powerful leader was soon to take them to the fabled land, where marvelous riches would be theirs.

Genghis Khan took nothing for granted, however. His realm had been won with great difficulty; neighboring lands would remain quiet only as long as he was all-powerful. If he were to be defeated in another

China's walled cities forced Genghis's army to refine its techniques of siegecraft. The domination of China required the full strength of Mongolian forces and nearly five years of difficult fighting.

country, far from the Mongol territory, some of the tribes he had subdued would undoubtedly rise up and devastate his country. The word *Mongol* would be a name of honor no more.

Since the days when he lived in hiding with his small brothers, his mother, and her feeble servant woman, Genghis Khan had been able to grasp the full import of whatever situation presented itself. He was not one to deny reality or to give in to paralyzing fear, nor did he ever attempt to avoid confronting difficulties through idle daydreaming. Rather, he analyzed the problems that lay before him and came up with solutions that were brilliantly inventive—yet utterly logical.

He decided that Hsi Hsia, the country that was perhaps most likely to betray him if he was defeated by the Qin, was now so weak that war was extremely unlikely at the moment. Yet he knew that some chieftains in his own country might be allied with him only because they were forced to be and that these warriors might join with other ambitious men in Mongolia or in the lands beyond its frontiers.

Genghis Khan's solution to this uncertainty was simple: he would take the tribal chieftains along with him, and all their male relatives and warriors as well. Mongolia would be left only with women, children, and the elderly and would be protected by a small army of 2,000 soldiers.

Throughout the three days and three nights that Genghis spent fasting in the solitude of his tent, he prayed to the Eternal Blue Heaven for blessings while he sought to avenge his forebears, whose blood had been shed by the vicious Qin rulers. He asked not only for the aid of good spirits but also for the assistance of evil spirits, for they were immensely powerful, too. When he finally walked out of his tent on the fourth day and spoke to his warriors, cheers rang out again and again. Genghis Khan said that Heaven had granted him victory.

Genghis had planned well in choosing springtime for the 450-mile march from the Kerulen to the Chinese border. After the army crossed the mountains, it had to make its way through the eastern part of the Gobi desert. But since the snows were melting at this time of year, water was available in the Gobi, as was dry fodder for the army's horses and the cattle it would use for food.

The Mongol scouts, who rode ahead of the army in a fan-shaped formation to watch for campsites and water as well as for the enemy, reached the Great Wall in several weeks. The Ongut tribe to the north of the wall allowed the Mongols to pass; previously, Genghis had reinforced the alliance with the Onguts by arranging marriages between his family and the Ongut leader's.

Behind the scouts rode five hordes of about four divisions (10,000 men) each, commanded by Genghis's three eldest sons — Juchi, Jagatai, and Ogatai — and by Jebei, the khan's chief commander, and Genghis himself. His youngest son, Tuli, rode with him in order to learn more about the art and science of war. As always, Genghis's arrow messengers kept him constantly informed about the progress of the others, and unlike most leaders of that time, Genghis ordered his messengers to report the

Mongol warriors ridicule Chinese forces with a display of trick riding. The Mongols overcame overwhelming odds with battlefield strategies based on surprise.

THE BETTMANN ARCHIVE

A 20th-century Mongol soldier stands beside a horse, his trusted ally in combat. The vastly superior horsemanship of Genghis's forces kept the enemy scattered.

bad news as well as the good. When dire reports were presented to him, he put the information to practical use and did not punish the bearer. But the Qin emperor in his capital at Beijing had been given inaccurate information about Genghis's advance. Since messengers were punished unless they brought good news, the emperor seldom was told the truth.

The invasion of China demonstrated the soundness of Genghis Khan's tactics. Although the Chinese forces far outnumbered Genghis's riders, thanks to the superb training and vastly superior mobility of the Mongols the nomads were able to keep the Chinese occupied with the defense of their most important areas while other Mongol warriors moved out in three directions to keep the enemy scattered. The Mongols were helped by warriors of the Mongol race who had been in the Chinese army but deserted as quickly as they could. More assistance came from desperate Chinese peasants who felt such rage and hatred for their emperor that they rose up against the Qin as soon as the Mongols appeared.

> ***As my calling is high, the obligations incumbent upon me are also heavy; and I fear that in my ruling there may be something wanting.***
> —GENGHIS KHAN

The ruling classes in China had exploited the people mercilessly. Although China's culture was hundreds of years ahead of other world civilizations at the time, the society was degenerate and decaying. Government officials were so corrupt that according to one student of China children were routinely included in the tallies of taxpaying adults; as a result, the people were so ruthlessly taxed that in desperation many began murdering their own babies in order to avoid paying additional sums. The peasants' fields were depleted because of relentless pressure to produce; the printing process was developed to its high degree in China not in a quest for dispensing knowledge but to print money to meet the nobility's unceasing demand for funds. Everywhere the peasants were landless and starving, harvests were failing, wealthy families were seizing whatever they wished without regard for the law.

In the teeming cities life was very different. Industry was thriving, thanks to slave labor. Workshops produced finely crafted goods, beautiful items that went to court officials and importers abroad.

Despite widespread desertion and insurrection by Chinese soldiers, however, the emperor's army was so immense that the war itself was long and difficult. In every campaign the Mongols used the strategy of dividing and marching in separate units that would later come together at a prearranged spot, where they all would fight together. Genghis Khan used the tactic — and the element of surprise — to perfection.

The first campaign against the Qin was in 1211. Although Genghis's own horde crossed the Great Wall and then surprised and overwhelmed the Qin

They eat the flesh of no matter what animal, even dogs and swine. They open a vein in their horses, and drink the blood. They cross every ravine and swim their horses over the rivers.

—anonymous contemporary description of the Mongols

army between the Hwang Ho River and the mountains and devastated the northwestern province of Shansi, the Mongols for some time were still unable to conquer the well-defended walled cities. Finally, however, Jebei's army took several fortresses strategically placed along paths to Beijing.

The fortifications of the capital city were impressive. By one account, Beijing's walls were 40 feet high, 40 feet wide at the top, and 50 feet wide at the base. The city was surrounded not by one but by three moats, and 900 towers, well stocked with soldiers, stood outside the walls, in addition to four forts. Hundreds of thousands of soldiers were defending Beijing, and Genghis knew that his forces were not ready to take the city. He allowed his horses to run free on the plains outside the capital with no resistance at all from the Chinese and remained there for a month until all the grass had been consumed. Then he withdrew his armies and camped north of the wall for the winter. His forces spent the long months practicing new approaches to siegecraft that had been devised by Genghis after much study.

China's many fortified cities provided Genghis's hordes with abundant opportunities to refine their techniques, and the new siegecraft system proved extremely effective. Genghis used a huge, mobile siege train made up of pack animals and wagons bearing weapons, supplies, equipment, and contraptions for firing missiles over the cities' walls. By promising excellent benefits of service as well as severe consequences for anyone who did not cooperate, the khan persuaded superb Chinese engineers who were prisoners of war to help in the production of Chinese-style weapons and to teach him new techniques of warfare. One historian claims that the engineer corps under Genghis Khan was every bit as skilled as those of Julius Caesar and Alexander the Great.

Whenever possible Genghis took towns by storm; if his armies were unable to sweep in at once, the siege train, accompanied by a division of warriors, would attack the wall and those defending it in an attempt to break through and at the same time to

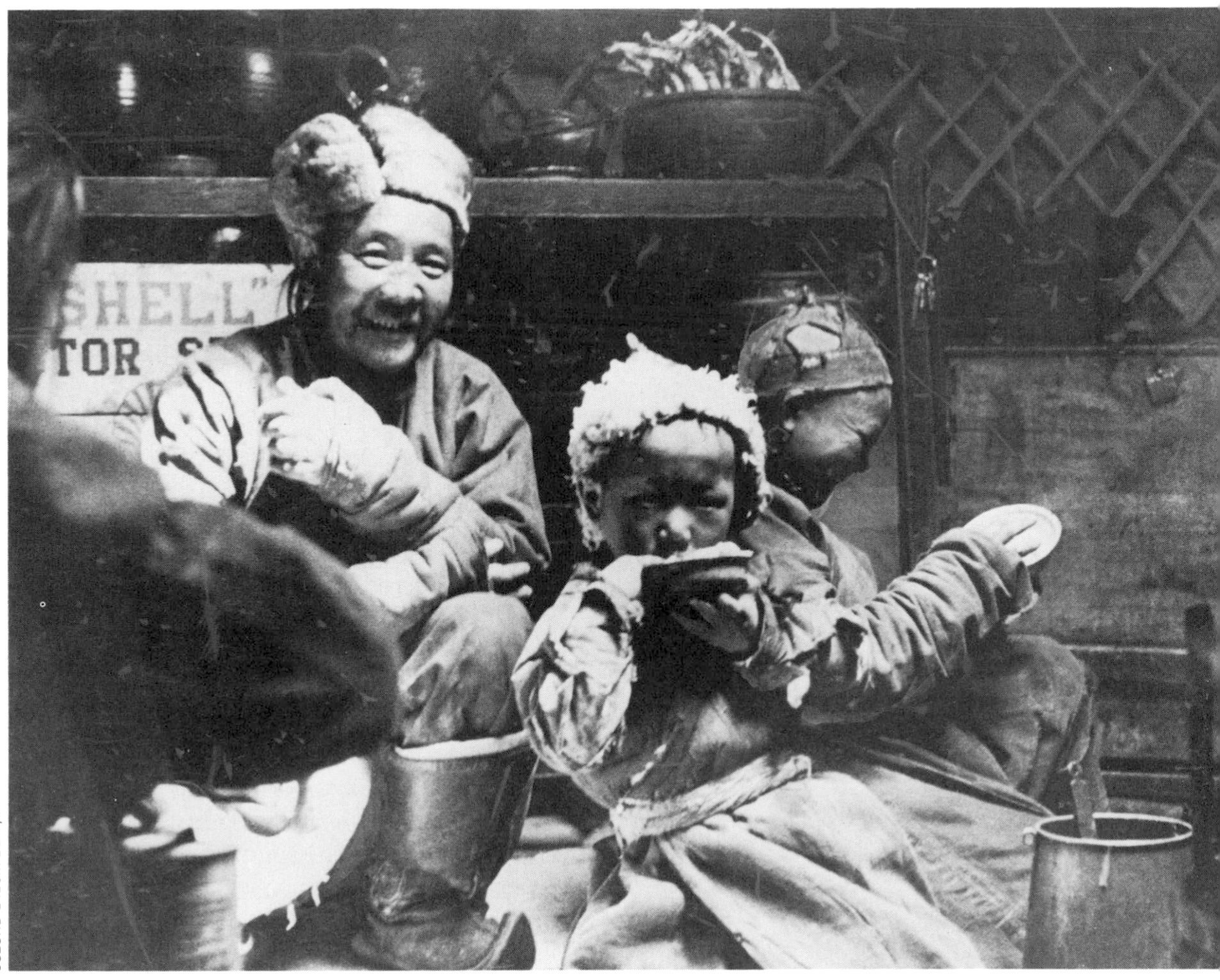

AP/WIDE WORLD PHOTOS

This Mongol family enjoys the same simple foods that were staples during the days of Genghis Khan. Goat cheese and the milk of mares and camels are the basis of the traditional Mongol diet.

kill as many of the enemy as possible. The siege train shot fiery missiles as the Mongols tried to scale the walls and surprise the soldiers; often Genghis's men seized entire sections of a city before the defenders recovered sufficiently to resist. If a city surrendered, Genghis was seldom harsh with its people; if the population continued to fight, the entire city would be destroyed in the ruthless manner for which the khan became notorious.

The huge siege train with its battering ram, catapults for missiles, and other instruments of war was but one part of Genghis Khan's extremely adaptable, perfectly coordinated, altogether formidable war machine. The commander in chief plotted

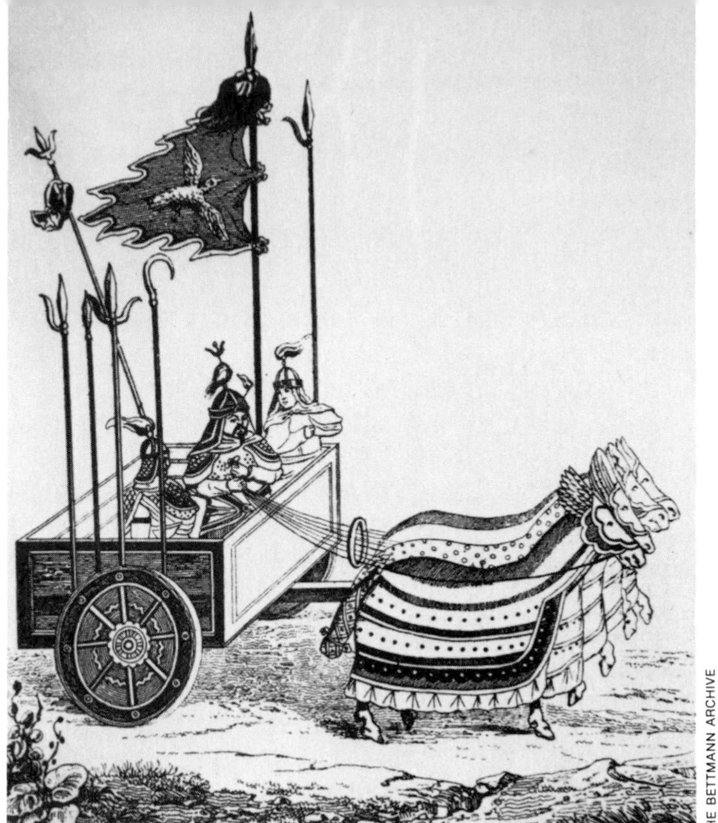
THE BETTMANN ARCHIVE

The Qin armies used heavy war chariots in their battles with the Mongols. Captured Chinese engineers helped the Mongols develop effective siege devices, including battering rams with explosive ends, attack ladders, and a variety of catapults and missiles.

every battle in minute detail beforehand, basing his plans on detailed information gathered by an efficient network of spies who ventured deep into enemy territory, usually disguised as traders or merchants. Genghis trained his field commanders — including his four sons and his companions Sabutai and Jebei — to be highly resourceful and effective without him. Thus, they could accomplish their goals as the unfolding situation dictated as long as they followed Genghis's overall strategy. They remained in close touch with their leader, however, through the arrow messengers.

Another of Genghis's innovations was the use of black and white signal flags by regimental commanders to control the movements of their armies. Messages thus were communicated instantly. When the flags couldn't be seen because of darkness or obstructions in the natural terrain, flaming arrows were substituted.

Genghis Khan used highly effective psychological warfare, as well. Before every campaign his spies spread rumors about the slaughter and destruction caused by the Mongol barbarians. A lot of the propaganda was accurate, of course, but again, devastation was not inevitable, since the Mongols often were lenient with enemies who cooperated — particularly those who had useful skills. At any rate, the fear campaigns without doubt helped weaken the enemy's will to resist.

Supplies were obtained for the huge army by appointed commanders, who oversaw the seizure of animals, food, equipment, clothing, and people from the country under attack. Genghis's own administrative staff was made up in large part of Chinese officials, doctors, and scholars who were captured during the assault on Hsi Hsia and the early struggles with the Qin.

After two years of patient effort, Genghis began to win decisive victories against fortress-cities and towns throughout the land. In just one of many similar battles, his troops caused so much bloodshed that the fields around the unfortunate city

These pieces, decorated with red glaze, are rare examples of 13th-century Chinese porcelain. Genghis Khan's successful armies brought the treasures looted from China back home with them.

XINHUA NEWS AGENCY

THE BETTMANN ARCHIVE

For centuries, cities in the northeastern area of China known as Manchuria were besieged by "barbarians" such as the Mongols. Genghis Khan consolidated control over the region in the early 13th century.

were still littered with human bones a decade after the surrender.

Throughout the fall and winter of 1213 the Mongols ravaged the entire Qin territory with the exception of the nearly impregnable city of Beijing. Genghis thus not only gained grazing land for his horses and additional practice in siegecraft for his men but also weakened the empire considerably. His armies had overpowered 90 fortified towns, leaving disease and famine to follow in the wake of the devastation. His forces killed thousands of people and captured thousands more, who were forced to work for the army as it stormed through the countryside, destroying farms, sacking towns, massacring the peasantry, setting fire to crops, and gathering loot along the way. The booty was then handed over to the friendly Onguts, at the edge of the steppe beyond the Great Wall, for safekeeping.

A man's greatest work is to break his enemies, to drive them before him, to take from them all the things that have been theirs, to hear the weeping of those who cherished them.
—GENGHIS KHAN

In March 1215 Genghis learned that the emperor had abandoned the capital city, located as it was dangerously close to the steppes. Many of the soldiers accompanying the fleeing ruler had turned back and were ready to swear allegiance to the Mongols.

Genghis judged that the time was right to take Beijing at last. He was longing to return to Mongolia after his absence of more than three years; indeed, his messengers had brought accounts of unrest in the border regions of western and southwestern Mongolia.

He also worried that leaders of lands that he had subdued might rise up against him while he was occupied in northern China. On the other hand, he was well aware that to leave China too soon would be to undo all he had accomplished. Knowing that the enemy behind Beijing's walls was severely weakened by dissension and poor morale, Genghis ordered his men to attack.

Though Beijing was considerably smaller than it is today, it was one of the largest cities of the 13th century and was surrounded by a 26-mile-long wall with 12 closely guarded gates. The Mongols managed to set the entire metropolis on fire and took away valuable silks, precious jewelry, gold, silver,

Genghis Khan receives a subject after his triumphant return from the campaign in China. The people of the steppes were elated by the return of their leader and his armies.

THE BETTMANN ARCHIVE

and thousands of extraordinarily talented craftsmen. The treasures and prisoners were sent in a seemingly endless procession of caravans to Genghis's temporary camp in Ongut territory, where the khan had retired to escape the oppressive heat of the Chinese summer.

Genghis Khan remained at his camp for approximately two years after the fall of Beijing. During this time he directed the organization of a military government in the enormous new regions that were coming under his rule. One of the prisoners was a scientist and scholar who had been working for the Qin. Genghis made the official, whom he judged to be both wise and honest, an adviser on the reorganization of the northern Chinese provinces. Having had no experience at all with a functioning urban economy, Genghis knew of nothing else to do with a city than to pillage and destroy it, but the administrator — named Yeliu Ch'uts'ai — convinced Genghis that the provinces could be governed in a way that would be to the benefit of both the Mongols and the Chinese. On Yeliu Ch'uts'ai's recommendation, Genghis established a system of taxation that replaced the usual destructive Mongol raids on conquered territories. He then appointed Mukuli, who had been his chief commander in the east since the time the mighty Mongol army was organized, to be his viceroy and the supervisor of the two Mongol tumans remaining in China. He knew he could count on Mukuli to carry on while he returned to Mongolia. Although the Mongols occupied the territory north of the Hwang Ho River, as well as present-day Manchuria and Korea, and Mukuli systematically occupied town after town, the Qin were not completely defeated until 1234, seven years after Genghis's death.

When Genghis Khan returned to his camp beside the beautiful Kerulen River after his five-year absence, he brought more than enough slaves to serve every Mongol and enough booty to make every family wealthy. The steppes were again populated with men, and joyous celebrations of the glory of the Mongol nation and its mighty khan of khans continued unabated for weeks. Truly the nomads believed with Genghis that "a man's greatest joy is to conquer and drive his enemies before him, to ride his horses and to take his possessions."

Now, in temporary repose on the tranquil grasslands, Genghis could consider problems that lay ahead. Former foes had gathered strength in his absence; new ones would create new crises. He was 54 years old, and though he couldn't know it, he faced yet another challenge — one that would consume the remainder of his enormous strength.

兀太祖
鐵木眞

7

The Final Battle

> ***When a man has achieved great power, what is there left for him to achieve but more power? When he has overcome all his enemies, what does he find but more enemies?***
>
> —R. P. LISTER
> historian, on Genghis's later years

Genghis was seated on a magnificent embroidered rug in his tent one afternoon, conferring with several of his closest advisers, when he heard the shouting of men and women, the terrified squeals of children, and what seemed to be the neighing of all the horses that ever lived under the Great Blue Sky. The din grew louder, and then one of his servants, shouting, asked to be admitted to the khan's tent. Genghis yelled for him to come in and asked what was the matter.

The servant backed halfway out of the tent and motioned toward the excited throng. A perspiring Mongol, one of the khan's ablest warriors, stepped forward carrying something that, despite its horrible dark blue-gray pallor and coarse black hair matted with dark crusts of blood, was unmistakably a human head.

Genghis Khan had never seen the unfortunate person, but he was certain that the head belonged to Guchluk, the brutal ruler of Kara Khitai. Several weeks earlier, Genghis had decided to send the commander Jebei with 20,000 riders to kill Guchluk. The late Guchluk was a Naiman prince whose father had fled from Genghis Khan in 1208 and had been given shelter by the khan of the Kara Khitai. Guchluk later married the khan's daughter and in 1211 thanked his father-in-law for his kindness by im-

Challenges from rebellious subjects confronted the aging khakan. These uprisings, issues of succession, and new campaigns vied for his attention in his final years.

SOVFOTO

EASTFOTO

A fresco from Genghis Khan's mausoleum chronicles the events of his life. Genghis surveys a map of his extensive domains as his court looks on in joy and reverence.

prisoning him and declaring himself khan. The self-appointed monarch ruled harshly and closed the Muslim temples. Guchluk persecuted the Muslims relentlessly and was despised by these unfortunate subjects, who made up most of the urban population in Kara Khitai.

Twenty thousand warriors were not many to send into such a vast land, but Genghis had been told by his spies how much the people hated Guchluk, and he knew that his warriors would meet little resistance. He had instructed Jebei to reopen every mosque he came upon and to tell the people that the warriors were marching against their oppressor and that they had nothing to fear from Genghis Khan. He was hoping to end the upheaval in Kara Khitai, for many of the nation's people had sent him gifts and pleas for help — despite the fact that Guchluk had murdered anyone even suspected of treason. Genghis also wanted to stop Guchluk's threats to one of the khan's greatest allies: the Uighur nation to the southwest of Mongolia.

The warrior who stood before Genghis Khan now, holding the grisly evidence of Jebei's triumph, informed the Mongol ruler that Kara Khitai had been subjugated in only a few weeks and that the high-pitched whinnying sound that could be heard above the excited shouts of the people outside the khan's tent was evidence of a magnificent tribute. As a present for the khan, Jebei's men had captured 1,000 of the highly prized white-muzzled horses of Kara Khitai. No finer steeds existed anywhere, and the Chinese had been importing the valuable animals for centuries. On every count that afternoon Genghis Khan was well pleased.

Kara Khitai was not the last land in the western part of the Asian continent to occupy Genghis Khan's attention. To the west of Kara Khitai was the formidable new empire of Khwarezm, which had been established in the area of the ancient Persian Empire by a Turkish shah, Ala ad-Din Muhammad. The Khwarezmian Empire was made up of most of the present-day countries of Iran, Afghanistan, and Pakistan and the huge region of the Soviet Union known as Turkistan.

Genghis Khan was not at all interested in waging war against Shah Muhammad; rather, the Mongols needed peacetime trade with the west by an overland route, since maritime trade had stopped because of disputes between ports on the Persian Gulf. The nomads needed many items brought by the Muslim merchants: metal helmets, shields, chain armor, silks, magnificent carpets, fine glass utensils, and jewelry.

In 1217 Genghis dispatched several messengers to Shah Muhammad, noting that he had conquered China and the nations to the north and needed no other lands and that trade between the two empires would benefit all concerned. Late in the same year the shah and the khan signed a treaty providing for continuation of the age-old trade route from the Mediterranean Sea to China.

The goodwill was short-lived. In order to initiate steady trade between the Muslim world and eastern

Asia, Genghis Khan sent a caravan to the Khwarezmian Empire. The great procession, headed by prominent Muslims and a special Mongol envoy, included 500 camels with a cargo of precious metals, silks and fine fabrics, furs, and beautiful objects made by Chinese craftsmen. The caravan was accompanied by agents representing each of Genghis Khan's princes, nobles, and generals. These envoys carried money for the purchase of Khwarezmian goods. No sooner had the Mongol caravan reached the Khwarezmian frontier, however, than it was stopped by the governor of the province. All the treasures, their cash, and the camels were seized, and nearly 200 people, including Genghis's personal representative, were killed.

Genghis named his third son, Ogotai (seated on throne), as his heir because of the young man's ability to get along with others. The Mongols captured much of eastern Europe during Ogotai's 12-year reign.

Though Genghis was shocked and enraged that the shah would break the agreement permitting caravans to move freely, he kept his anger in check and simply sent a group of ambassadors in protest and to demand that the shah punish the offending governor. Ala ad-Din Muhammad, however, took great offense because the infidel dog of the nomads had presumed to judge one of his own governors.

The shah then ordered that the leader of the delegation be killed. In so doing the shah declared war on the Mongols — an astonishingly stupid decision. The medieval Asian kingdom Muhammad ruled was in a state of decay; its social and political structures were crumbling. At one time the society had been agricultural, managed by landowner-aristocrats who functioned as landlords. It was their responsibility to develop irrigation, build canals and bridges, maintain buildings and equipment, and to look after the well-being of the people. But gradually huge commercial centers gave rise to a wealthy class of traders who lived in fortified castles on tremendous estates, cut off from the people in the countryside. At the same time, the military class grew stronger and the Muslim clergy, the administrators who ran the kingdom, became increasingly powerful. The ordinary people were valued only as taxpayers; the agricultural areas were neglected, and famine plagued the land.

The Khwarezmian army was supplied with luxuries, and the lavish courts were maintained — and yet money was so scarce that what food was available for the peasants was nearly impossible to buy. Uprisings were common: in 1212, for example, people in the city of Samarkand rebelled. They murdered many Khwarezmians and hung the bodies in the markets for butchering. The shah's response to such insurrections was swift and bloody.

After the shah had Genghis Khan's chief ambassador put to death, he then added insult to the injury: he ordered the beards of the other envoys shaved and the men sent back to the khan in humiliation.

Ancient chronicles relate that Genghis wept when he learned of the murder and saw how his ambas-

Say ye unto the Khwarezmians that I am the sovereign of the sunrise, and [he is] the sovereign of the sunset. Let there be between us a firm treaty of friendship, amity, and peace, and let traders and caravans on both sides come and go.

—GENGHIS KHAN
to an ambassador from the Khwarezmian empire

sadors had been insulted. "The powers of the Eternal Blue Heaven know that I'm not the cause of this terrible misfortune," Genghis cried. Then he shouted, "May the Eternal Blue Heaven help me to find energy for revenge." The war had begun.

Genghis was about to enter unknown territory. All his battles had been waged in regions with which he was at least to some extent familiar — the wars on the steppe, the great campaign in northern China. Genghis knew that the Khwarezmian sultans had armies that far outnumbered his. He was understandably uneasy.

One of his wives, Yesui, finally said what must have been on the minds of everyone who was close to Genghis. "You are the khan of khans," she told him, "and it is fitting that you should ride into new worlds. But all creatures have to die. What will become of your people if something should happen to you? Which of your four sons do you designate your heir — Juchi, Jagatai, Ogotai, or Tuli? Your sons, your brothers, your own people, are wondering about these things."

Genghis pondered Yesui's words and then praised her courage. He turned to Juchi, his eldest, and asked him for his opinion. But before Juchi could speak, Jagatai, who was extremely jealous of his brother, burst out: "Father, you can't want to name Juchi as your successor! He is the son of the Merkit warrior who carried off his mother!"

Juchi grabbed Jagatai by his shirt. "Our father has never treated us differently; how dare you to talk as you do? You are not superior to me!" he shouted.

"I challenge you!" he went on. "If you beat me with bow and arrows, I will cut off my thumb. If you beat me in wrestling, I will stay where I fall!"

Genghis Khan reprimanded Jagatai and forbade him ever again to speak as he just had. Jagatai then apologized and suggested that neither he nor Juchi be Genghis's heir but rather their younger brother, Ogotai — a young man known for his generosity and his sensible ways. Genghis approved of the idea.

The year was 1219. Genghis Khan was ready to confront the other half of the Asian continent. He

ART RESOURCE/BILDARCHIV FOTO

An overland route to the West was required for access to items, like this helmet, supplied by Muslim traders. Wars erupted despite Genghis's desire to concentrate on the peacetime needs of his people.

sent his arrow messengers to summon warriors from the farthest reaches of his domain. In preparation for his assault, he assembled an army of some 250,000 men and mobilized a huge siege train, complete with flamethrowers, catapults, and battering rams. Then, in order to divert the Khwarezmians' attention from the main Mongol forces in the north, he ordered Jebei and his son Juchi to advance with 30,000 men through a pass in the Tien Shan Mountains that was covered with five feet of snow.

Genghis then sent four parts of his army to surprise the Khwarezmians by attacking from four different directions. The forces then laid siege to the city of Otrar, home of the governor who had seized Genghis's caravan the year before. The enemy fought with the desperation that came from the

CULVER PICTURES

Kublai Khan, grandson of Genghis, became khakan and emperor of China. His military strategies and cultural interests redirected the broad sweep of Mongol influence back to its origins in the Orient.

knowledge that no one captured would survive, and the battle lasted nearly six months.

When the Mongols finally broke through the walls of Otrar, they found the governor on a roof, throwing tiles at Genghis's men because he had run out of arrows. The doomed man was sent to the khan, who ordered that his eyes and ears be filled with molten silver and that he then be killed by slow torture.

The campaign was conducted brilliantly. At one point the Mongol forces, led by the khan himself, suddenly appeared at the city of Bukhara, where they took a garrison of some 30,000 Turkish warriors completely by surprise. The enemy never dreamed that an army could cross 400 miles of the totally barren desert that had been in the Mongols' path.

At another city, the townspeople and warriors watching the arrival of the Mongol hordes advancing from every direction were astounded at the size of Genghis's army — which actually was fewer than 200,000 men at that point. Genghis had cunningly ordered that the thousands of prisoners captured in previous battles march in formations, carrying the Mongol standards. The enemy mistook their captive countrymen for nomad warriors.

The khan's riders pursued Ala ad-Din Muhammad for approximately 2,000 miles over nine long months, until the arrogant, foolish man died in January 1221, exhausted from his ordeal.

The shah's violent actions against the Mongols, ironic in light of Genghis's original peaceful intentions, surely rank among the great mistakes of history. Muhammad's belligerence set off a series of events leading to the Mongol conquest of the Khwarezmian Empire, another invasion of Hsi Hsia, subjugation of the last provinces of the Qin and the Song empires in China, and finally, under Mongols in the decade after Genghis's death, the invasion and conquest of eastern Europe.

As Genghis's hordes moved westward, they stormed and subjugated the great cities of Bukhara, Samarkand, Urgenj, and later numerous cities in the Crimea and South Russia, with massive shows of force. In one encounter the Mongols brought 3,000 machines to hurl lances, 300 catapults, 700 machines to throw burning naphtha (a highly flammable petroleum-based liquid), and 4,000 ladders.

Far more terrifying than the amassed weaponry, however, was the Mongols' legendary savagery. In one city taken by force the inhabitants were divided up among the warriors for slaughter. One old woman cried out that if she was spared she would

The city of Samarkand was part of the empire of Ala ad-Din Muhammad. In 1212 the residents rebelled against his harsh rule and killed many Khwarezmians.

TASS FROM SOVFOTO

AP/WIDE WORLD PHOTOS

This modern-day Mongolian monk embraces the same simple, mystical faith expressed by Ch'ang Ch'un, the Taoist monk from whom Genghis hoped to learn the secret of eternal life. Ch'ang disappointed Genghis in this respect but impressed him with his teachings about the importance of simplicity and moderation.

give the soldiers a pearl. When the men agreed, she said she had swallowed it. The Mongols killed her, cut her stomach open, and found not one but several gems. Genghis promptly ordered that the stomachs of all the dead be slit on the chance that they, too, might have swallowed pearls.

The Mongols laid siege to one town for two weeks and then broke through the walls and rounded up 70,000 men, women, and children. The prisoners were shot with arrows. The hordes also were merciless with the land itself. As they moved through the countryside they destroyed the oases that had been so carefully cultivated to sustain orchards, gardens, vineyards, cornfields, and rice paddies. The Mongols demolished dams, reduced palaces to rubble, and burned crops. They knocked down the carefully placed screens of trees that protected the crops from sandstorms and undid the accomplishments of millennia, turning everything to ruins and barren acreage.

In the Khwarezmian town of Nishapur the Mongols took terrible revenge on the inhabitants, some of whom had slain Genghis Khan's son-in-law a few months before. After the Mongols scaled the walls and opened the gates, 10,000 warriors accompanied Genghis's grieving daughter into the center of the city so that she could witness a four-day-long slaughter of nearly everyone and everything, including dogs and cats. Only 400 people were spared — highly skilled craftsmen who would be able to perform important work in Mongolia.

> ***All who surrender will be spared; whoever does not surrender but opposes with struggle and dissension, shall be annihilated.***
>
> —GENGHIS KHAN
> during the war with the Khwarezmian empire

To be certain that no townspeople survived by lying motionless among the dead, Genghis's son Tuli ordered that every body be decapitated and that the heads be stacked in three piles: men's, women's, and children's. Despite the gory carnage, Genghis Khan and his followers believed that they were behaving justly and appropriately. They were punishing the Khwarezmian people in the only way they knew for ravaging the caravan and preventing the trade between nations that had been agreed upon. Thus it was that Genghis Khan could be shockingly brutal in war but fair, generous, compassionate, and essentially moral with his own people.

After the conquest was complete, Genghis let it be known that he wanted to learn about the lands he had desolated. Two scholarly Muslims, men of law and government, offered to carefully instruct him about cities and how to administer them profitably. As always, Genghis was an excellent listener and a ready student, and he eventually appointed the men administrators, along with Mongol associates, of the ancient cities. He had begun to take on the responsibilities of managing his new acquisitions, and he handled this new task with intelligence and skill.

At about the same time, the khan took up the matter of his death. In 1219 he sent for a renowned Taoist monk in north China called Ch'ang Ch'un, a man who reportedly knew the secret of eternal life. The khan must have been terribly disappointed after convincing himself that the mystical philosopher would tell him how to live forever and arranging to have the old man escorted across the vast distance between their homes. Nevertheless, Genghis showed no dismay; instead, in keeping with the noble side of his character, he thanked the monk, bestowed an honorary title on him, and ordered tents set up for the visitor a short distance from the royal tent. Genghis also accepted with good grace the monk's refusal to kneel before him, his rejection of *kumys*, the Mongols' national drink, and his negative reply to the khan's invitation to dine with him every day.

The barbarian conqueror listened raptly to the otherworldly teachings of Ch'ang Ch'un, who emphasized the "force without name" that moves the world and the ideals of simplicity, purity, and moderation. Genghis asked the old man about such important matters as his empire, the difficulties of governing, and how best to preserve his kingdom. He summoned his sons to hear the teachings and instructed his prime minister, Yeliu Ch'uts'ai, to interpret and to record the monk's words both in Chinese and Mongolian.

The simplicity and directness of the sage appealed to Genghis Khan, who hated pomposity and arrogance. One historian tells of the contempt the khan had for the elaborate rituals and formal manners of the Persian and Chinese aristocracies. When a male secretary who had been in the court of Ala ad-Din Muhammad and was used to interpret and to write messages in Persian or Arabic wrote at Genghis's request a warning letter to a ruler in the west, the man unfortunately couched the threat in flowery language. The fancy phrases were part of Persian tradition, but when they were read aloud Genghis suspected he was being mocked. Since he could not be sure one way or the other, he had the man put to death, just in case.

Genghis asked his princes to call him by his given name, Temujin, and he allowed no title to be used on his documents. He retained his respect for loyalty and courage rather than immense power and wealth, and he respected above all the ways of the nomad—the life that was his as a young man.

One day something happened that shook the newly contemplative khan to the tips of his boots. He had joined his sons and several close companions in a hunt and was pursuing a wounded boar when the beast turned and charged. Genghis raised his bow but suddenly toppled from his horse. Then, to the utter amazement of all, the boar stopped and stood still, gazing at Genghis without moving. Then the animal turned and ran off.

Genghis was appalled at having fallen from the horse and was shocked that such a thing could have happened to a rider as skilled as he was — after all,

THE METROPOLITAN MUSEUM OF ART, THE HARRIS BRISBANE DICK FUND

Hunting scenes used to illustrate Persian poetry of the Mongol era. A hunting accident led to the mighty khan's death. He gave orders that the news of his death should be suppressed until Mongol troops finished subduing a revolt in Hsi Hsia.

Despite all expectation, the time of my last campaign and of my passing is near. I wish to die at home. Let not my end disarm you, and on no account weep for me, lest the enemy be warned of my death.

—GENGHIS KHAN
last words to his military commanders

he had spent most of his waking hours since early childhood on horseback. On top of everything, Genghis knew that a wild boar that refrained from killing after starting to charge was unheard of, and he was extremely uneasy.

The prime minister, Yeliu Ch'uts'ai, explained that Genghis had been warned by heaven not to take such chances with his life. Genghis then asked for Ch'ang Ch'un's opinion. The philosopher declared that the time had come to forgo difficult activities like hunting. Regrettably, Genghis did not pay sufficient attention to his advisers' words as the years wore on.

During this time, Jebei and Sabutai had been marching through Persia, into Georgia, over the Caucasus Mountains and into the Russian steppes. They sacked some of Persia's grandest cities, destroyed villages and crops, and ultimately defeated and slaughtered a Russian army. Then, late in 1222, they moved to the northeast and massacred the Bulgar people in the city of Kazan. When they finally returned to Genghis, who was resting in the region of Ulan Bator in Mongolia, they brought him information that his sons would use 20 years later in an attack on Europe. The generals had covered more than 5,000 miles, defeating a dozen separate peoples along the way. On the other hand, although the two gifted warriors vanquished every opponent in Persia and across the Caucasus, the lands were not completely conquered, strictly speaking, since the local leaders did not swear loyalty to Genghis Khan, nor did they come under Mongol rule. The warring led by Jebei and Sabutai from 1220 until 1222 was more like a violent raid; definitive conquest was accomplished by Genghis's children and grandchildren.

After less than a year back in the familiar camping grounds of the Tula River, the aging khan was forced to go to battle once more. The leaders of the remaining Qin forces in China and the Tanguts in Hsi Hsia had united against him, intending to recover lands lost earlier. In the spring of 1226, when Genghis was 64, he left with 180,000 warriors to break the alliance and establish Mongol supremacy once more. As he headed southeast with his men, he disregarded warnings he had heard from the Chinese wise man and threw himself into a hunt for wild animals. He was thrown by his horse and suffered severe internal injuries. That night he developed a high fever, and his generals immediately suggested that they return home long enough for the khan to recover. Genghis refused, however, declaring that he would not have the enemy saying that the Mongols were weak. The warriors took several cities in the summer and fall and by December were nearing the capital of Hsi Hsia.

As they advanced, they struggled to stave off the Tangut cavalry. Suddenly, in a move typical of Genghis's style of warfare, the Mongols fell back upon the ice-covered Hwang Ho River, and the enemy followed. Because the Tanguts' horses were shod in iron, the animals slipped and slowed to a hesitant walk. Genghis's men immediately counterattacked, their shoeless horses moving with relative ease on the frozen surface. At the same time the Tanguts still on the bank were attacked from behind by another Mongol division.

The warriors moved on to conquer the capital city, after which they planned to march east to strike at the Qin. In the late spring of 1227, however, Genghis was feeling terribly ill and had to stop and make camp. He allowed only his chief counselors and his family to know of his failing health.

Genghis ordered that when the Qin were finally defeated, the emperor was to be killed and his people put to death or enslaved. But he asked that when he died the news be kept secret until the conquests were complete and homage had been paid with gifts.

Then Genghis summoned his children and grandchildren, gave each an arrow, and told them to break it. "That is what will happen to you if you try to go through life alone," he said. Next, he removed a great quantity of arrows from his spare quiver and asked each to try to break the bundle. No one could do it. "If you stay together," he said, "and help one another, do not trust enemies, and follow my code of laws, you will be safe."

In August 1227 Genghis Khan died quietly in his

THE BETTMANN ARCHIVE

The 14th-century Mongol chieftain Tamerlane tried to revive the glories of Genghis Khan's empire in western Asia. Although Genghis Khan is often associated with violent cruelty, Tamerlane far surpassed the earlier Mongol leader in terms of savagery.

EASTFOTO

The restored mausoleum of Genghis Khan as it appears today, near the mountain where he had hidden as a youth. During his funeral procession, every living thing that crossed the mourners' path was killed in tribute to their fallen leader.

mountain camp. He was 65. In his last hours he reaffirmed the appointment of his son Ogotai to rule as khan. Though the young man lacked the iron will and the tenacity of Jagatai and was unable to control the drunkenness that Genghis had always detested, Ogotai knew how to listen closely to others and to use what he learned. And although Ogotai didn't have the military genius and the wild energy of Tuli, the youngest son, he was able to get along with everyone he met and could manage the most difficult of men. Since none of his sons had all the attributes of their father, Genghis designated the one to be khan who was perceptive, kind, and a student of men.

Following Genghis's death, a thousand nobles and their warriors clustered around the wooden cart that held his body, and as they started the long journey to Mount Burkan Kaldun, where Genghis had asked to be buried, the people stayed so close together that no one could see the vehicle in the center of the crowd. As they took Genghis's corpse over mountains, through forests, across deserts and streams, the Mongols maintained absolute silence and, according to custom, killed every living thing they encountered along the way.

By this time, the Mongol Empire stretched from

the Black Sea east to the Sea of Japan, from the Black Sea south to the Arabian Sea, and then northeast along the Indus River and east across China. Genghis had inaugurated a new era of trade routes and vast land empires. His descendants — Ogotai; Kuyuk, son of Ogotai; Mangu, son of Genghis's son Tuli, and Tuli's third son Kublai — continued what Genghis had so spectacularly begun. They marched against the Song Empire in southern China and against Korea, western Asia, northern Russia, Poland, Germany, and Hungary. In 1294 the empire was at its peak, having steadily expanded in every direction since 1227. It included one-half of all living human beings.

With Heaven's aid I have conquered for you a huge empire. But my life was too short to achieve the conquest of the world. That task is left for you.
—GENGHIS KHAN
to his sons at the end of his life

Genghis's armies destroyed irreplaceable aspects of civilization in Asia and were responsible for terrible slaughter. Yet thanks to his constructive efforts, not all the effects of the Mongol conquest were negative. Great roads were opened and maintained throughout the empire, and Genghis encouraged the growth of free trade along land routes that were well maintained and safe by day and by night. In addition, though Genghis had never seen the sea, a tremendous maritime trade was established with India. A world market was created that thrived for more than a century, and one respected historian writes that he has no doubt that such important features of civilized life as the technique of printing, the compass, and firearms did not originate in Europe but rather were brought in from the Far East due to the Mongol influence. Subsequent Asian leaders such as Tamerlane were significant, but the legacy of Genghis Khan is a profound one.

To this day, Mongol tribes make annual pilgrimages to the sacred mountain where Temujin hid as a youth and to which he returned at crucial times to pray.

Genghis was buried beneath a solitary tree near the peak while a thousand riders kept watch below. In the years that followed, saplings sprang up around the trunk; today, the area is covered by an impenetrable forest of larches, cedars, and pines — protecting forever the final resting place of the khan of khans.

Further Reading

Charol, Michael. *The Mongol Empire: Its Rise and Legacy.* London: George Allen and Unwin, 1940.

Dupuy, Trevor Nevitt. *The Military Life of Genghis, Khan of Khans.* New York: Franklin Watts, 1969.

Lamb, Harold. *Genghis Khan, Emperor of All Men.* Darby, PA: Darby Books, 1981.

Lister, R. P. *Genghis Khan.* New York: Stein and Day, 1969.

Martin, H. Desmond. *The Rise of Chingis Khan and His Conquest of North China.* Baltimore: The Johns Hopkins Press, 1950.

Waley, Arthur, ed. *The Secret History of the Mongols.* New York: Barnes and Noble, 1964.

Chronology

1162	Birth of Temujin
1175	Betrothal of Temujin to Bortei
	Death of Temujin's father, Yesugei the Brave
ca. 1177	Temujin and his brother murder their half brother
1179	Briefly captured by Targutai
	Marries Bortei
1180	Merkits raid Temujin's camp; he abandons Bortei
	Temujin wins Bortei back after an expedition against the Merkits
1183	Named khan and given the name of Genghis
1201	Genghis defeats Jamuga's army
1203	Defeats Togrul and Jamuga at the Battle of Mount Jeje'er
1204	Defeats Naiman army at Chakirma'ut
1206	Proclaimed khan of khans
1207	Invades the Tangut state of Hsi Hsia
1209	Hostilities with Hsi Hsia end with the payment of a tribute from the emperor
1211	Genghis begins campaign against the Qin Empire; the Mongols cross the Great Wall of China
1215	Conquers Beijing
1217	Guchluk is beheaded in Kara Khitai; his kingdom comes under Mongol rule
	Khwarezmian leader Ala ad-Din Muhammad breaks a commercial treaty with Genghis and kills a Mongol ambassador
1219	Genghis declares war on the Khwarezmian empire
1226	Embarks on a campaign to break the alliance between the Qin and the Tanguts
	Falls from his horse and is severely injured
Aug. 1227	Death of Genghis Khan

Index

Afghanistan, 93
Ala ad-Din Muhammad, 93, 95, 98, 102
Alexander the Great, 82
Altai (mountains), 63
anda, 39
Arabian Sea, 107
Baikal, Lake, 63
Beijing, 73, 80, 82, 87, 88
Bektor (half brother), 23, 31, 32
Belgutai (half brother), 23, 31, 32, 33, 36, 41, 43
Black Forest, 38, 43
Black Sea, 19, 107
Bogurchi, 36–38, 41, 64
Bortei (wife), 27, 38, 41, 43, 44, 46, 47, 51, 57
Bukhara, 98
Burkan Kaldun, 43, 106
Caucasus Mountains, 104
Chakirma'ut, Battle of, 57, 58
Ch'ang Ch'un, 101, 102, 104
China, 18, 19, 20, 24, 59, 69, 72, 75, 80, 81, 82, 87, 93, 96, 98, 104, 107
Crimea, the, 98
Crusades, the, 19
Dai Sechen, 26–29, 38
Genghis Khan
  birth, 24
  campaign against Merkits, 43, 44
  clan chief, 32, 35, 36, 37, 39, 41, 43, 44, 46
  conquers Hsi Hsia, 70–72
  death, 105, 106
  early years, 24, 25, 27, 31, 32
  invasion of China, 78–83, 85, 87
  khakan (khan of khans), 62, 63, 64, 69, 70, 71, 75, 77, 92, 93, 94, 95, 102
  khan, 47, 48, 49, 57, 59, 61
  kills half brother, 32
  law code of, 63, 64
  military system of, 52, 53, 65, 66, 67, 68, 71, 83, 84, 85
  war with Khwarezmian Empire, 96, 97, 98, 101
Georgia, 104
Germany, 107
Gobi Desert, 17, 63, 71, 73, 78, 79
Great Wall of China, 18, 25, 26, 57, 59, 69, 73, 74, 77, 78, 81, 87
Guchluk, 91, 92
Hoelun (mother), 14, 23–25, 29, 30, 31, 32, 33, 38, 39, 44, 46, 47
Hsi Hsia, 59, 69, 70, 71, 72, 73, 78, 85, 98, 104, 105
Hungary, 107
Hwang Ho (Huang Ho) River, 71, 82, 89, 105
India, 107
Indus River, 107
Iran, 93
Jagatai (son), 79, 96, 106
Jamuga Sechen, 44, 47, 49, 51–59, 62
Japan, Sea of, 107
Jebei, 79, 82, 84, 91, 92, 93, 97, 104
Jelmi, 39, 41, 67
Jochi Darmala, 51
Juchi (son), 44, 46, 79, 96, 97
Julius Caesar, 82
Kara Khitai, 59, 75, 91–93
Kasar (brother), 24, 31, 33, 36, 41, 43, 55
Kazan, 104
Keraits, 39, 49, 53–54
Kerulen River, 77, 78, 89
Khaji'un (brother), 24, 33, 41
Khalakhaljit, Battle of, 53
Khingan (mountains), 63
Khwarezmian Empire, 20, 75, 93–98, 101
Korea, 89, 107
kowtow, 73
Kublai (grandson), 107
Kulan (wife), 57
kumys, 102
Kuyuk (grandson), 107
Manchuria, 89
Mangquts, 52
Mangu (grandson), 107
Mediterranean Sea, 93
Merkits, 13, 14, 41, 43, 44, 51, 56, 57
Mount Jeje'er, Battle of, 55
Mukuli, 89
Munlik, 28, 29
nadom, 43
Naiman, 55–57
Nakhu Bayan, 36–38
Nishapur, 101
noyon, 21
Ogatai (son), 79, 96, 106, 107
Onguts, 79, 87, 88

Onon River, 13, 14, 31, 35
Orhon River, 44
Otrar, 97, 98
Pakistan, 93
Persia, 72, 104
Persian Gulf, 19, 93
Poland, 107
Qin Empire, 20, 25, 52, 59, 69, 73, 75, 77, 78, 80, 81, 85, 87, 89, 98, 104, 105
quran, 52
Russia, 98, 104, 107
Sabutai, 84, 104
Samarkand, 98
Selenga River, 44
Sengun, 53, 55
Shansi province, 82
Silk Road, 72
Song dynasty, 75, 98, 107
Sorgan Shira, 35
Soviet Union, 93
Taichar, 51
Tamerlane, 107
Tanguts *see* Hsi Hsia
Targutai, 32–34, 36
Tatars, 24, 27, 52, 53, 55
Tatatungo, 57, 63
Tayan, 57
Temuga (brother), 24, 33, 41
Temulin (sister), 24, 41
Tien Shan Mountains, 97
Togrul, 39, 43, 44, 49, 52–55, 57, 67
Tula River, 104
Tuli (son), 79, 96, 101, 106, 107
tuman, 44
Tunguses, 15
Turkistan, 15
Turks, 15
Uighurs, 55, 57, 93
Ulan Bator, 14, 104
Urgenj, 98
Uru'uts, 52
Volohai, 70, 71
Wei Wang, emperor of China, 73, 74
yasak, 63, 64
Yeliu Ch'uts'ai, 89, 102, 104
Yellow River *see* Hwang Ho River
Yesugei (father), 13, 14, 21, 23–28, 32, 35, 39, 54
Yesui (wife), 96

Judy Humphrey is a writer and editor based in New York.

Arthur M. Schlesinger, jr., taught history at Harvard for many years and is currently Albert Schweitzer Professor of the Humanities at City University of New York. He is the author of numerous highly praised works in American history and has twice been awarded the Pulitzer Prize. He served in the White House as special assistant to Presidents Kennedy and Johnson.